More Praise for *Sustainable Happiness*

"What makes *Sustainable Happiness* such an important collection is the book's practicality. It helps readers understand ways they can make things better for themselves and their communities starting now."
—**David Brancaccio, host, American Public Media's *Marketplace Morning Report*, and co-executive producer, *Fixing the Future***

"I read this book with both sadness and gladness. Sadness to realize how far astray global culture has led us from the true sources of happiness, and gladness that there are so many wise and practical voices gathered in one book to guide us back to lives of real fulfillment."
—**Margaret J. Wheatley, author of *Leadership and the New Science***

"These stories of enjoyable forms of supportive local cooperation stimulated by wider individual frames of reference make concrete what 'sustainable happiness' means. Try it. It's easier than you may think."
—**Ralph Nader, author and public interest advocate**

"Everyone's life is a balancing act in the often-difficult world. This enlightening anthology offers a trove of helpful reflections on what it really means to have and to be, reminding us that joy is there to be found."
—**Mollie Katzen, chef and author of the *Moosewood Cookbook***

"*Sustainable Happiness* is a fine selection of thoughtful articles. You'll come away with a deeper understanding of how we can improve the quality of all of our lives while passing on a verdant planet to our descendants. I heartily recommend this book!"
—**John de Graaf, author and cofounder of the Happiness Alliance**

"The *Sustainable Happiness* volume delivers inspiration for your personal journey of joy and well-being as you navigate 'the pursuit of happiness' in a deeply troubled world. Read this book for the wisdom it contains. It will nourish your soul."
—**Parker J. Palmer, educator and author of *Let Your Life Speak* and *A Hidden Wholeness***

"We've been sold a bill of goods about happiness—and it's costing us in all the things that make life worth living. *Sustainable Happiness* shows that the hours of our lives are not trinkets but rather a gift from and for the living world. You'll be happy you read this book."
—**Vicki Robin, bestselling author**

"Finally, a book on 'the pursuit of happiness' that is not self-referential and small minded! Instead, it is honest, challenging, and invitational to a larger world beyond the small self. What a magnificent collection of writers and ideas!"
—**Fr. Richard Rohr, OFM, founder of the Center for Action and Contemplation**

"What the happiness movement needs now is actionable examples pointing the way for our future that are rooted in the 'us,' not just the 'me.' *Sustainable Happiness* is the first book to answer that call."
—**Laura Musikanski, author and executive director, Happiness Alliance**

"*Sustainable Happiness* offers a gentle invitation to return to our deeper humanity, to a place that isn't so bogged down in daily chores, minute-to-minute texts, and a brain full of clutter. *I loved it!*"
—**Dee Williams, author and tiny house builder (cofounder of Portland Alternative Dwellings)**

"In *Sustainable Happiness*, YES! has offered us a rich buffet of facts that surprise, ideas that inspire, stories that touch our hearts, and much food for thought. And really, who doesn't want to be happy?"
—**Lama Tsomo, author of the forthcoming book *Why Is the Dalai Lama Always Smiling?***

"The wealth of *Sustainable Happiness* grows out of the wisdom that has guided the beautiful growth of *YES!* initiatives—invariably, a celebration of ordinary people setting daily examples of courageous commoning, step-by-step, with infinite patience yet a necessary sense of urgency."
—**Madhu Suri Prakash, writer and educator**

"*Sustainable Happiness* blazes a trail into the brave new world of transforming extremely materialistic development models into ones that create true prosperity and happiness and of changing consciousness. A great book!"
—**John Perkins, bestselling author of *Confessions of an Economic Hit Man***

"Modern society is a network of lures intended to seduce and reduce 'humans' to 'consumers.' Dig into *Sustainable Happiness*. Join the revolution of perception. Your happiness depends on it."
—**Makana, musician, composer, and activist**

Sustainable
Happiness

Sustainable Happiness

Live Simply, Live Well, Make a Difference

Edited by Sarah van Gelder
and the staff of YES! Magazine

BK

Berrett–Koehler Publishers, Inc.
San Francisco
a BK Life book

www.yesmagazine.org

Berrett-Koehler Publishers, Inc.
1333 Broadway, Suite 1000
Oakland, CA 94612-1921
Tel: (510) 817-2277 Fax: (510) 817-2278 www.bkconnection.com

Ordering Information
Quantity sales. Special discounts are available on quantity purchases by corporations, associations, and others. For details, contact the "Special Sales Department" at the Berrett-Koehler address above.
Individual sales. Berrett-Koehler publications are available through most bookstores. They can also be ordered directly from Berrett-Koehler: Tel: (800) 929-2929;
Fax: (802) 864-7626; www.bkconnection.com
Orders for college textbook/course adoption use. Please contact Berrett-Koehler:
Tel: (800) 929-2929; Fax: (802) 864-7626.
Orders by U.S. trade bookstores and wholesalers. Please contact Ingram Publisher Services,
Tel: (800) 509-4887; Fax: (800) 838-1149; E-mail: customer.service@ingrampublisherservices
.com; or visit www.ingrampublisherservices.com/Ordering for details about electronic ordering.

Berrett-Koehler and the BK logo are registered trademarks of Berrett-Koehler Publishers, Inc.

Printed in the United States of America

Berrett-Koehler books are printed on long-lasting acid-free paper. When it is available, we choose paper that has been manufactured by environmentally responsible processes. These may include using trees grown in sustainable forests, incorporating recycled paper, minimizing chlorine in bleaching, or recycling the energy produced at the paper mill.

Library of Congress Cataloging-in-Publication Data
Sustainable happiness : live simply, live well, make a difference / edited by Sarah van Gelder and the staff of *YES! Magazine*. — First edition.
    pages cm
Includes bibliographical references and index.
ISBN 978-1-62656-329-2 (pbk.)
1. Happiness. 2. Simplicity. 3. Conduct of life. 4. Environmentalism. 5. Sustainable living.
I. Van Gelder, Sarah. II. *YES!* (Bainbridge Island, Wash.)
BJ1481.S876 2014
170'.44—dc23   2014028808

FIRST EDITION

19 18 17 16 15 14   10 9 8 7 6 5 4 3 2 1

Cover design: Nicole Hayward
Cover photo: asife/Shutterstock
Interior design and composition: Leigh McLellan Design
Copyediting: *YES! Magazine*

Dedicated to our friends
folk music legend Pete Seeger (1919–2014)
and civil rights icon Vincent Harding (1931–2014)
who spent their lives working to make happiness
accessible to everyone.

Contents

PART TWO The Practice of Happiness
(or, How You Can Get Some)

Maybe it shouldn't be a surprise, but our readers tell us they love the happiness features in *YES! Magazine* and on www.yesmagazine.org, and they share these articles widely. *Sustainable Happiness: Live Simply, Live Well, Make a Difference*, contains some of our—and their—favorite pieces on happiness.

This book considers the evidence about the nature of real happiness. Sustainable happiness, it turns out, multiplies as it's shared; it blossoms when individuals, families, communities, and the natural world are thriving.

If you're looking to enrich your life and deepen your happiness, this book offers research-based practices. If you'd like to reweave the fabric of relationships in your community, you'll find here some of the best, most practical visionaries on this topic. And if you'd like to see our society prioritize the well-being of the natural world and of people—including those too often left out—you will find resources for organizing and activism.

For years, *YES!* has published stories that touch on all of these aspects of happiness. Our very first issue, in 1996, was about the freedom that comes from turning away from excessive consumerism, which is a time sink for families, a driver of inequality for our society, and an ecological burden for the planet. Since then, we've published issues on the good life, the new economy, sustainable sex, new livelihoods, happy families, and sustainable happiness. Our all-time most popular article was "10 Things Science Says Will Make You Happy" (Chapter 2).

When we started scanning the archives of *YES! Magazine* and yesmagazine.org for articles to include in this anthology, we were overwhelmed by the choices. Even in the last days of producing this manuscript, we were still rediscovering articles and essays we would have loved to include. You can find many of them via links at www.yesmagazine.org/happiness-book.

The fact that there is so much to choose from is a tribute to those who have contributed to *YES!* and to this volume (see a full list of contributors at the end of the book). And it's a tribute to the talented group of editors who found and cultivated these writers and worked with them to develop the powerful stories that make up this book, including Tracy Loeffelholz Dunn, Christa Hillstrom, Brooke Jarvis, Madeline Ostrander, Doug Pibel, Valerie Schloredt, and James Trimarco.

YES! web editor Christa Hillstrom led the editing of the chapters that make up this volume with the help of former senior editor Madeline Ostrander. Tracy Loeffelholz Dunn, *YES!* creative director, first suggested the idea for this book and worked closely with Berrett-Koehler's design team on photographs and the cover. Susan Gleason, *YES!* media and outreach manager, helped manage this project, aided by interns Jim McGowan and Dana Drugmand. Interns Liz Pleasant, Molly Rusk, and Laura Garcia pitched in to proofread, as did print editors Valerie Schloredt and Doug Pibel, who also helped track down citations and rights. Rod Arakaki, audience development director, encouraged us all along the way, as did Fran Korten, *YES!* executive director. Dean Paton joined our staff as executive editor just in time to take major responsibility for the magazine, freeing up enough of my time to write the introductions and edit this book.

YES! Magazine is only possible because of the extraordinary group of people who help make our nonprofit publication thrive. In addition to those listed above, the *YES!* staff includes Cloantha Copass, Jing Fong, Derek Hoshiko, Miles Johnson, Paula Murphy, Rebecca Nyamidie, Yvonne Rivera, Audrey Watson, and Michael Winter. We are grateful to our board of directors and to the 5,000-plus donors who make this work possible.

This book is our second collaboration with Berrett-Koehler Publishers, a "for benefit" B Corporation we have come to deeply appreciate for their professionalism and integrity. A special thanks to Steve Piersanti, Berrett-Koehler's president and publisher, who offered guidance and editorial feedback from the beginning; Jeevan Sivasubramaniam, editorial managing director, who helped us stay on track; and all the others who worked with us to make this book a success.

We also want to thank some of the leaders on this topic who have offered advice and content, including On the Commons, the Center for Investigating Healthy Minds, ServiceSpace.org, and The Greater Good Science Center at the University of California, Berkeley; also John de Graaf, co-founder of the Happiness Alliance, and Steve Arnold, a leader in the realm of social and emotional learning. All have inspired us and contributed lovingly and substantively to *YES!* and to this book.

Sarah van Gelder
Co-Founder and Editor in Chief
YES! Magazine
Suquamish, Washington
June 2014

Saint Martin's Island, Bangladesh (Photo by Mohammad Moniruzzaman)

How We Lost Track of Real Happiness
and Where to Find It Now

Sarah van Gelder

In the last 100 years, we got very confused about happiness. This is no small thing. The way we define happiness drives what we do, what we're willing to sacrifice, and how we spend our money and our time.

This confusion didn't just happen. Advertisers spend billions spreading the illusion that more stuff will bring us happiness. And policy wonks of all political stripes—but especially those connected to business interests—spread the message that economic growth leads to well-being. Both are false promises that have instead been undermining the very conditions that could lead to sustainable happiness.

Sustainable happiness is built on a healthy natural world and a vibrant and fair society. It is a form of happiness that endures, through good and bad times, because it starts with the fundamental requirements and aspirations of being human. You can't obtain it with a quick fix; sustainable happiness cannot be achieved at the expense of others.

The good news is that sustainable happiness is achievable, it could be available to everyone, and it doesn't have to cost the planet. It begins by assuring that everyone can obtain a basic level of material security. But beyond that, more stuff isn't the key to happiness.

It turns out that we don't need to use up and wear out the planet in a mad rush to produce the stuff that is supposed to make us happy. We don't need people working in sweatshop conditions to produce cheap stuff to feed an endless appetite for possessions. We don't even need economic growth, although some types of growth do help.

The research shows that sustainable happiness comes from other sources. We need loving relationships, thriving natural and human communities, opportunities for meaningful work, and a few simple practices, like gratitude. With that definition of sustainable happiness, we really can have it all.

A Short History of American-Style Happiness

Consumption has not always been king in the United States. It became a national preoccupation beginning in the 1920s when business leaders began worrying that Americans were satiated, that they had all the appliances and consumer goods they wanted.[1] Executives and pro-business politicians thought the economy would stall if people chose to spend time enjoying life rather than working more and buying more.

So the advertising industry joined forces with Freudian psychologists to channel our desires—to link the universal wish for status, love, and self-esteem with the new "Gospel of Consumerism."[2]

"Wants are almost insatiable," claimed President Herbert Hoover's report on the economy, published just months before the 1929 crash. "One want satisfied makes way for another.... We have a boundless field before us; there are new wants that will make way endlessly for newer wants, as fast as they are satisfied…by advertising and other promotional devices, by scientific fact finding, by a carefully predeveloped consumption a measurable pull on production has been created…it would seem that we can go on with increasing activity."[3]

The modern advertising industry systematically set out to redefine our beliefs about happiness. Freudian psychoanalyst Ernest Dichter is one of those who joined forces with the advertising industry. "To some extent," he said, "the needs and wants of people have to be continuously stirred up."[4]

Their strategy works. Today, an iPad, the right vacation, or the latest sneakers have become prerequisites for getting respect. Certain brands of beer are synonymous with friendship and a sense of community. An oversized house points to status and proof of your earnings and ability to provide for a family. These are all, of course, ideas created by advertisers whose clients profit when we buy more than we need.

But buying all this stuff has real consequences. Houses today are, on average, twice as large per person as they were 40 years ago.[5] The burden of debt for those extra rooms and deluxe finishes lasts for decades. Some get addicted to the buyer's high that follows a big purchase, but the initial exuberance spikes and disappears quickly. The debt, the extra work hours required to pay it off, and the resulting time away from friends and family go on and on.

Exhausted by long hours working and commuting, people begin to wonder what happened to real happiness. Advertisers are there with the answer: You just need to spend still more on plastic surgery, antidepressants, or a new car. The average child in the United States sees between 50 and 70 ads a day on television[6]; the average adult sees 60 minutes of ads and promotions a day.[7]

For the working poor, those on limited incomes, and the unemployed, much of the stuff that advertisers claim will bring happiness is out of reach, making the false promises a cruel joke. For all income levels, but especially for the poor, advertising becomes a relentless reminder that one is falling short of what others have—and of the good life.

"Who tells the stories of a culture really governs human behavior," said media scholar George Gerbner. "It used to be the parent, the school, the church, the community.... Now it's a handful of global conglomerates that have nothing to tell, but a great deal to sell."[8]

The conversation about sources of fulfillment and joy has been colonized by the advertisers that manufacture the mindset of the consumer culture.

Paying the Price for Cheap Stuff

The workers who make and distribute our stuff are among those who pay the price for our consumer lifestyle. When people lack money, but are told that more stuff is essential to their happiness, low prices become paramount. Local businesses are driven into bankruptcy by big-box stores that can slash prices by paying rock-bottom wages.

Production workers find themselves unwilling participants in a race to the bottom for the lowest wage. Employers pick up and relocate if wages and safety standards are lower somewhere else or if workers begin organizing a union.

The nonhuman life of the planet suffers, too, from the colossal ecological burden of producing all our stuff. Human activity is causing species to go extinct at 1,000 times the rate that would otherwise occur in nature, according to a recent study published in *Science*.[9] Industrial chemicals turn up in the bodies of sea mammals in the Arctic—and in our own bodies. A giant patch of plastic garbage circulates in the Pacific Ocean, poisoning wildlife up and down the food chain. Most troubling of all are the effects of burning massive quantities of fossil fuels and clear-cutting and burning forests. The carbon saturating the atmosphere is turning the ocean acidic and overheating the planet. The disruption of the climate threatens our coastlines, food supplies, and sources of fresh water, and supercharges wildfires and massive storms.

Growth No Longer Delivers Happiness

More consumption was supposed to bring happiness to us as individuals, and likewise, economic growth was supposed to bring well-being to society as a whole.

The postwar period was considered an economic success story, and especially in the '60s and '70s, it was a time when many were lifted out of poverty and the gap between rich and poor was much smaller than it is today. The growth of the economy as measured by Gross Domestic Product (GDP) rose steadily.

But the GDP is an untrustworthy measure. It gauges economic activity, whether or not that activity means improvements. Dig a strip mine and sell the metals, minerals, or coal, and the GDP will thank you—even if you pollute the drinking water for thousands. Raise fresh food in your garden, share it with friends and with the local homeless shelter, and stay healthy and happy, and the GDP doesn't budge.

The Genuine Progress Indicator (GPI), on the other hand, measures overall well-being; it subtracts out harmful things like crime, illness, farmland loss, and declining water quality, and adds in contributions to the economy that the GDP doesn't count, like unpaid work in the home and volunteering in the community.

Until 1979, GDP and GPI both increased in the United States, more or less in tandem. But after 1979, something different happened. The GDP continued growing, while the GPI stalled. More and more of our time and resources were invested in economic growth, but it was no longer delivering happiness, especially for those still stuck in poverty.

Why did the size of the economy continue to grow while well-being stagnated?

The culprits are "a rising of income inequality combined with environmental and social costs rising faster than consumption-related benefits," says Ida Kubiszewski and colleagues in a paper published in *Ecological Economics*.[10]

In other words, we're not getting much happiness for all the time, money, and natural resources we're using—and the benefits are going mostly to those at the top.

What changed? Among other things, free trade agreements and pro-corporate governments now make it possible for transnational corporations to outsource production to the lowest-wage regions of the world with the fewest regulations guarding worker and environmental safety. That strategy keeps prices down. But it makes it easy for corporations to slash good jobs and exploit workers here and internationally. The poverty wages and abuse of farmworkers in the United States, the numerous factory fires and the collapse of the Rana Plaza building in Bangladesh, the suicides at the Chinese factories that make Apple products, and the blood diamonds in the Congo are just some examples of the high price paid by those who produce our stuff.

Productivity has risen throughout the postwar era, especially with the deployment of computers and robotics. More is now produced with an hour of worker time than ever. The increased income from that productivity could have been shared with workers in the form of higher pay or fewer hours for the same pay. Or the profits could have been taxed to fund higher education, infrastructure upgrades, a high-speed transportation system, a transition to a green economy, or any number of other things that would increase sustainable happiness. Instead, companies used the increased productivity to lay off workers, offer huge compensation packages to executives, purchase other companies, and pay out high returns to wealthy stockholders. And they spent billions on lobbyists and campaign contributions to win favorable laws, reduced taxes and regulations, and sweetheart trade deals. Organized labor no longer has enough clout to negotiate for a share of the increased income; wages have stagnated since the '70s, while the income and assets of the top 1 percent—and especially the top 0.1 percent—have skyrocketed.

A Diminished Quality of Life

The dominance of this profit-driven economy is undermining our quality of life.

To get by in an age of stagnant wages and government indifference, Americans work longer and longer hours. Those at the bottom of the income ladder, especially single parents, often work two or three jobs to bring in enough to get by, and many live in poverty even while working full-time. With long hours (plus long commutes), who has time to be happy?

This form of corporate-driven consumerism increases inequality and undermines family life, and it's gobbling up the natural resources of our planet. Mountaintops are blown off, forests converted to tar-sands open-pit mines, and farmland converted into fracking drill sites and strip malls. The planet has limits—a reality overlooked by those who preach unending economic growth. We now have industrial chemicals in our water supply, Dust Bowl-style droughts, acidifying oceans, dying bee colonies, melting polar ice, and extreme hurricanes and fire storms. There's a saying, "If mama ain't happy, ain't nobody happy." Mother Earth is not happy.

Many people are concerned about these issues, of course. But ordinary people don't have the resources to get the attention of elected officials, who must raise millions of dollars to run national campaigns. A recent study[11] by two prominent academics, slated for publication in the Fall 2014 *Perspectives in Politics,* confirms that the United States has become an oligarchy. The views of ordinary people and their advocacy groups have virtually no effect on policy, the study found. Yet economic elites and organizations representing business interests have "substantial independent impacts" on government policy.

This is how inequality undermines sustainable happiness. The promise that more stuff brings happiness turns out to be a false promise. Likewise, the claim that the rising tide of economic growth "lifts all boats" is also false.

So Where Can We Find Sustainable Happiness Now?

If economic growth and consumerism aren't a recipe for sustainable happiness, then how do we get it?

Sustainable happiness is a form of well-being that goes deep —it's not a fleeting sensation of pleasure or a temporary ego boost. Instead, it is enduring because it taps into our most authentic aspirations and involves building relationships and practices that support us through good times and bad (see Part 2).

Sustainable happiness is built on a mutually supportive community. It grows out of the recognition that our well-being is linked to that of our neighbors. When we know that we can count on others in difficult times, that there is a place for everyone, and that we can make a meaningful contribution and be recognized for it, we have the foundations of sustainable happiness.

And sustainable happiness grows out of a healthy living Earth. At a very basic level, it comes from recognizing that each drink of water, each breath of air, the food that grows out of the soil or comes from the waters—all is possible because of the living ecosystems of the planet. Sustainable happiness goes deeper, though, to a celebration of the natural world even when it is not offering us a direct benefit.

The good news is that sustainable happiness is compatible with a healthy environment, an equitable world, and our own fulfillment. And it is contagious—the things that create well-being for one person tend to be good for others and for all life.

Sustainable happiness is possible—but much depends on the choices we make individually and as a society. Here are some places to start: 1) Stop the causes of trauma and support healing, 2) Build economic and social equity, 3) Value the gifts we each bring, 4) Protect the integrity of the natural world, and 5) Develop practices that support our own well-being.

1. Stop the Trauma

Like the common-sense rule contained in the Hippocratic Oath, we could start by doing no harm.

Life inevitably brings some kinds of hurt: A relationship breaks up, a loved one dies, or a job fails to materialize. With support from friends and family, we recover and go on.

Yet there are types of trauma that can be debilitating for a lifetime and even across generations. And many are preventable.

Veterans suffer high rates of post-traumatic stress disorder (PTSD). According to the Department of Veterans Affairs, 30 percent of those treated in VA hospitals after returning from deployment in Afghanistan or Iraq have PTSD.[12] Their children also suffer and are more likely to be anxious or depressed.[13]

Sexual violence is another way large numbers of people are traumatized. An estimated one in five women will be raped over the course of her lifetime, and a third of rape survivors will experience PTSD. Survivors are also three times as likely to have an episode of serious depression.[14]

Nearly 700,000 children are subjected to sexual and physical abuse each year in the United States, according to the U.S. Department of Health and Human Services.[15] Children suffer disproportionately from poverty, which also causes lasting trauma.

And there are the intersecting traumas caused by generations of exclusion, economic dislocation, and violence directed at people of color, who experience higher rates of PTSD as a result of ongoing racism, according to research cited by Dr. Monica Williams in *Psychology Today*.[16]

Among the most important ways to create a happier world is to end the wars, abuse, and exclusion that are sources of continued trauma, and to support the healing of survivors.

2. Create Equity

Stress can be healthy, if it's the right kind. Short-term stress actually increases memory and mental function.[17] But chronic stress—especially stress caused by events over which we have little control—increases the risk of heart disease and the likelihood of death. The Whitehall Studies—the famous 20th-century investigations into the causes of death and disease among British civil servants—showed that low-status workers had a death rate three times higher than those in the upper reaches of the hierarchy, even when controlling for other class-based stress factors.[18] Moreover, the damage caused by inequality extends beyond the work place. Epidemiologist Richard Wilkinson has demonstrated that those living in unequal societies have many times higher rates of mental illness, homicide, and teen pregnancy (see Chapter 4).

So if we want healthier and happier lives, we need a more equitable society—fairer in both an economic sense and in terms of the empowerment we all have to determine our own lives.

3. *Value Everyone's Gifts*

It may be counterintuitive, but sustainable happiness comes from what we give, not what we take or even what we have. People who find their unique gift and are able to offer it to others are often happiest (see Chapter 14).

Cameron Anderson, a professor at the Haas School of Business at the University of California, Berkeley, published a study in *Psychology Science* that shows winning the respect and admiration of our peers matters more than having stuff. "You don't have to be rich to be happy, but instead be a valuable contributing member to your groups," says Anderson. "What makes a person high in status in a group is being engaged, generous with others, and making self sacrifices for the greater good."[19]

Likewise, research cited in *YES! Magazine* by Stacey Kennelly shows that our happiness increases when we have the respect of our peers, but not necessarily when we have a higher income or more wealth.[20]

College students who are politically engaged are happier, according to research by professor Tim Kasser. "Political activism scores were associated with feeling more pleasant emotions, reporting greater life satisfaction, and having more experiences of freedom, competence, and connection to others," he says in a *YES! Magazine* article, "Making a Difference Makes You Happy."[21]

4. Protect the Integrity of the Natural World

The natural world doesn't just bring us happiness; it is what makes life possible, and protecting its integrity contributes to sustainable happiness.

Getting out into nature improves our sense of well-being and is especially important for children. Benefits include reduced stress, improved health, more creativity, and better concentration, says Amy Novotney in the *Monitor on Psychology*.[22]

The illusion that humans are separate and apart from the living Earth is finally giving way to an understanding that our fate is tied to the fate of the planet on which we all depend (see Chapter 19). Our work to protect and restore the planet's ecosystems will mean clean water, healthy foods, a stable climate, and a better shot at sustainable happiness for generations to come.

5. Develop Practices That Support Our Own Well-Being

An egalitarian society that protects the natural world; minimizes war, racism, and abuse; and welcomes the expression of each person's unique gift provides the foundation for sustainable happiness. But we don't have to wait for the world to change. There are things we can do at home, too, that boost our own sustainable happiness.

We can exercise, a better cure than prescription drugs for much of what ails us. A sedentary life is as dangerous to health as smoking, according to studies cited by the American College of Sports Medicine.[23] Regular moderate exercise not only reduces the risk of heart disease, diabetes, and stroke; it also makes us happier, often controlling depression as effectively as prescription antidepressants.[24] It's much cheaper, and all of the side effects are good.

We can also develop a practice of gratitude (see Chapter 13) and learn to be mindful (see Chapter 7).

Some of the happiest people are those who have survived great illnesses or other major life challenges and have become conscious of the choices they make about their finite lives. There's something about facing the possible end of life that brings into focus the precious choice we have about how to spend our remaining days.

"Everything can be taken from a man but one thing: the last of human freedoms—to choose one's attitude in any given set of circumstances, to choose one's own way," Viktor E. Frankl wrote.[25]

A Global Happiness Reset

As endless growth and bottomless consumption lose their luster as aims for our lives, many people are seeking out better ways to achieve happiness. New approaches are beginning to take hold around the world.

Buen Vivir

Out of the indigenous regions of South America comes the idea of *buen vivir* (the good life). In this way of thinking, well-being does not just come from the individual pursuit of happiness. It comes from being part of a vibrant world that includes both human and natural communities.[26] Instead of serving the economy, the economy exists to serve us. We are here to live well with our families, and it is in relationships of respect and reciprocity with neighbors and with our ecological neighborhood that we will find happiness.

This, of course, is a radical reversal of the economic growth aims of society as promoted by both liberal and conservative political leaders. Instead of seeing nature and human labor as an input into a production machine we call the economy, this perspective aims to foster an ethic of stewardship, mindfulness of the interests of descendants seven generations on, gratitude for what we have—along with a sense of *enoughness*—and the acknowledgement of the rights of all life.

Buen vivir has now been embedded in the constitutions of Bolivia and Ecuador. This framework has inspired a grassroots approach to the climate crisis and has become the foundation of international discussions, especially in Latin America.

Bhutan's Gross National Happiness

In 1972, soon after ascending to the position of the Fourth Dragon King of Bhutan, the young Jigme Singye Wangchuck declared that he was more interested in gross national happiness than in gross domestic product. This statement launched studies and assessment surveys, based on Bhutan's unique culture and values, so that happiness could be used as a yardstick for policy-making in this small Asian nation. Gross national happiness as defined by Bhutan includes psychological well-being, health, education, time use, cultural diversity and resilience, good governance, community vitality, ecological diversity and resilience, and living standards.[27]

Focusing on the well-being of the people guided Bhutan as it followed its own path, rather than adhering to the interests of global economic forces. Bhutan decided not to join the World Trade Organization, for example, when it concluded that such a move would undermine happiness and well-being.

"If Bhutan joins the WTO, it surrenders, by very definition, the right to determine who participates in defining and achieving the happiness of the Bhutanese whole to external forces.... In other words, Bhutan surrenders to market forces and to the powers that are dominant in the market its own sovereignty," said Stanford history professor Mark Mancall.[28]

Bhutan's idea that happiness, not growth, should be the measure of progress is spreading. The United Nations General Assembly adopted a Bhutan-sponsored resolution in July 2011 that calls on other nations to make happiness and well-being a central feature of their development work, and to develop indicators to measure the well-being of their own people.[29]

The Happiness Movement in the United States

In the United States, the states of Maryland and Vermont are using the Genuine Progress Indicator to measure happiness. They are factoring in the benefits of volunteer time, housework, educational achievements, and functional highways and streets while subtracting things like crime and the depletion of nonrenewable energy sources. By measuring these and other factors, a more complete picture emerges of real well-being.

"If we look at things holistically, based on health, community connection, arts and culture, the environment, we will govern the country differently," John deGraaf, a co-founder of the Happiness Alliance, told me. "We will understand that success comes more in societies that are egalitarian, that have great time balance—short hours and shared work, strong social safety nets so people feel secure. We'll have greater confidence in government and greater trust in each other."

● ● ●

Maybe happiness sounds like a frivolous endeavor for us as individuals, and especially for governments and the United Nations, to pursue. But consider Thomas Jefferson's insistence on including the "pursuit of happiness," rather than "property," along with life and liberty in the Declaration of Independence. Jefferson was deeply influenced by the Greek notion of *eudaimonia*, which refers not to a fleeting pleasure but to the essentials of what it means to be human—in other words, to human dignity.

In this sense, sustainable happiness is not frivolous at all. There aren't enough resources in the world for all of us to live a consumer lifestyle. But by choosing wisely, we can have a world in which each of us can live in dignity.

Those who are affluent can gain happiness by eschewing excess consumption, de-cluttering, practicing gratitude, relishing good times with loved ones, and protecting the natural environment.

For those lacking the means to provide for themselves and their families, an increase in access to resources can result in real improvements in well-being.

As a whole, we stand to gain a lot. A more equitable world fosters trust, increasing our capacity to work together to solve the big problems of our time. It means a world with less crime, less disease, less corruption, and less waste. And it's a world in which we make the best possible use of the natural resources we extract from the Earth by making sure that—to loosely paraphrase Gandhi—our natural wealth goes to meet needs, not greed.

Ways of life that focus more on happiness and less on economic growth leave time for family, community, and the development of the many dimensions of our lives that we know bring real happiness.

One more thing: In a time of increasing disruptions related to a changing climate and economic dislocation, our challenge will be to create the conditions that encourage us to turn *to* each other in hard times, not turn *on* each other. We are far more likely to achieve that in a more equitable world, where we are mindful of the many blessings we have and skilled at discovering sources of happiness that don't cost the planet, but are abundant and free.

PART ONE

What We Know About Real Well-Being

Annual pillow fight at Union Square, New York City (Photo by Waisum Tam)

Introduction

We come into this world naked with nothing to count on but love.

Along the way, we pick up other ideas about what's important—status, possessions, a bucket list of experiences and accomplishments. But at the end of life, those who reflect back often return to seeing love as the source of real happiness.

Philosophers and religious leaders have long warned us not to get distracted by petty ambitions. "It is preoccupation with possessions, more than anything else, that prevents men from living freely and nobly," said British philosopher Bertrand Russell.[1] "No servant can serve two masters," Jesus says in Luke 16:13. "You cannot serve God and money."

The myth that we must fill up our lives with stuff is a lot like the myth that we must pursue unlimited economic growth: both beliefs harm people and the planet while obscuring the ingredients of real well-being.

In Chapter 1, author Roman Krznaric describes three societies that have embraced simple living instead of seeking material gain: our stone-age ancestors, ancient Greeks, and colonial-era Quakers. The philosophy of simple living, he writes, has shown up in almost every civilization.

But are these approaches outdated and even naïve? Where does happiness come from today? The research on "subjective well-being"—otherwise known as happiness—is clear, as cupcake baker and social justice activist Jen Angel describes in Chapter 2. Happiness comes from such simple things as appreciating everyday moments, making contributions to others, and treasuring time with family and friends.

The advertiser-driven notion of happiness still dominates our culture, though, and those who manufacture our stuff often pay the price. Many do dangerous, mind-numbing work for pay so low they can barely keep their families alive. When we break out of our identities as consumers, we can reclaim our identities as citizens, says Annie Leonard, head of Greenpeace USA, in Chapter 3. As engaged citizens, we find the personal power to push for everyone's rights and opportunities to pursue happiness.

Doing so would benefit those at the bottom of the income ladder. Epidemiologist Richard Wilkinson argues, though, that egalitarian societies make life better for everyone, rich and poor alike (Chapter 4). Trust is higher, crime is lower, and life expectancy is longer when there is greater equality. This perhaps should not surprise us since, according to science historian Eric Michael Johnson, we evolved to cooperate and share resources (see Chapter 5).

In our divided society, creating trust and solidarity takes conscious effort. Akaya Windwood, head of the Rockwood Institute, suggests in Chapter 6 that we start by taking a moment to acknowledge one another's humanity across divides of generation, race, and gender.

When our lives are imbued with a sense of *enoughness*, when we live in thriving human and ecological communities, and when we are free of the poverty associated with highly unequal societies, we have love and energy to spare. When our families, our neighbors, those we meet on the street, and the creatures of the natural world are also doing well, their happiness contributes to our own. It becomes a generative cycle. Sustainable happiness in one realm fosters well-being in all the other realms of life. Interconnectedness—love, even—is unleashed, not just at the beginning and end of life, but as a guide for our choices throughout.

CHAPTER 1

The Movement to Live Simply
Is Older Than You Think

Roman Krznaric

When Pope Francis first assumed office, he shocked his minders by turning his back on a luxury Vatican palace and opting instead to live in a small guest house. He has also become known for taking the bus rather than riding in the papal limousine.

Simple living is not about abandoning luxury, but discovering it in new places.

The Argentinian pontiff is not alone in seeing the virtues of a simpler, less materialistic approach to the art of living. In fact, simple living is undergoing a contemporary revival—in part due to the ongoing recession forcing so many families to tighten their belts; but also because working hours are on the rise and job dissatisfaction has hit record levels, prompting a search for less cluttered, less stressful, and more time-abundant living.[2]

At the same time, an avalanche of studies, including ones by Nobel Prize-winning psychologist Daniel Kahneman, have shown that as our income and consumption rise, our levels of happiness don't keep pace.[3] Buying expensive new clothes or a fancy car might give us a short-term pleasure boost. But this doesn't add much to most people's happiness in the long term.

It's no wonder there are so many people searching for new kinds of personal fulfillment that don't involve a trip to the shopping mall or online retailers.

Many people don't realize that simple living is a tradition that dates back almost 3,000 years, and has emerged as a philosophy of life in almost every civilization.

What might we learn from history's great masters of simple living as we rethink our lives today?

Eccentric Philosophers and Religious Radicals

Anthropologists have long noticed that simple living comes naturally in many hunter-gatherer societies. In one famous study, Marshall Sahlins pointed out that aboriginal people in Northern Australia and the !Kung people of Botswana typically worked only three to five hours a day.[4] Sahlins wrote that "rather than a continuous travail, the food quest is intermittent, leisure abundant, and there is a greater amount of sleep in the daytime per capita per year than in any other condition of society." These people were, he argued, the "original affluent society."

In the Western tradition of simple living, the place to begin is in ancient Greece, around 500 years before the birth of Christ. Socrates believed that money corrupted our minds and morals, and that we should seek lives of material moderation rather than dousing ourselves with perfume or reclining in the company of courtesans. When the shoeless sage was asked about his frugal lifestyle, he replied that he loved visiting the market "to go and see all the things I am happy without." The philosopher Diogenes—son of a wealthy banker—held similar views, living off alms and making his home in an old wine barrel.

We shouldn't forget Jesus himself who, like Guatama Buddha, continually warned against the "deceitfulness of riches."[5] Devout early Christians soon decided that the fastest route to heaven was imitating his simple life. Many followed the example of St. Anthony, who in the third century gave away his family estate and headed out into the Egyptian desert where he lived for decades as a hermit.

Later, in the thirteenth century, St. Francis took up the simple living baton. "Give me the gift of sublime poverty," he declared, and asked his followers to abandon all their possessions and live by begging.[6]

Simplicity Arrives in Colonial America

Simple living started getting seriously radical in the United States in the early colonial period. Among the most prominent exponents were the Quakers—a Protestant group officially known as the Religious Society of Friends—who began settling in the Delaware Valley in the seventeenth century. They were adherents of what they called "plainness" and were easy to spot, wearing unadorned dark clothes without pockets, buckles, lace, or embroidery.[7] As well as being pacifists and social activists, they believed that wealth and material possessions were a distraction from developing a personal relationship with God.

But the Quakers faced a problem. With growing material abundance in the new land of plenty, many couldn't help developing an addiction to luxury living. The Quaker statesman William Penn, for instance, owned a grand home with formal gardens and thoroughbred horses, which was staffed by five gardeners, 20 slaves, and a French vineyard manager.

Partly as a reaction to people like Penn, in the 1740s a group of Quakers led a movement to return to the spiritual and ethical roots of their faith. Their leader was an obscure farmer's son who has been described by one historian as "the noblest exemplar of simple living ever produced in America." His name? John Woolman.

Woolman is now largely forgotten, but in his own time he was a powerful force who did far more than wear plain, undyed clothes. After setting himself up as a cloth merchant in 1743 to gain a subsistence living, he soon had a dilemma: his business was much too successful. He felt he was making too much money at other people's expense.

In a move not likely to be recommended at Harvard Business School, he decided to reduce his profits by persuading his customers to buy fewer and cheaper items. But that didn't work. So to further reduce his income, he abandoned retailing altogether and switched to tailoring and tending an apple orchard.

Woolman also vigorously campaigned against slavery. On his travels, whenever receiving hospitality from a slave owner, he insisted on paying the slaves directly in silver for the comforts he enjoyed during his visit. Slavery, said Woolman, was motivated by "the love of ease and gain," and no luxuries could exist without others having to suffer to create them.

The Birth of Utopian Living

Nineteenth-century America witnessed a flowering of utopian experiments in simple living. Many had socialist roots, such as the short-lived community at New Harmony in Indiana, established in 1825 by Robert Owen, a Welsh social reformer and founder of the British cooperative movement.

In the 1840s, the naturalist Henry David Thoreau took a more individualist approach to simple living, famously spending two years in his self-built cabin at Walden Pond, where he attempted to grow most of his own food and live in isolated self-sufficiency (though by his own admission, he regularly walked a mile to nearby Concord to hear the local gossip, grab some snacks, and read the papers).[8] It was Thoreau who gave us the iconic statement of simple living: "A man is rich in propor-

tion to the number of things which he can afford to let alone."
For him, richness came from having the free time to commune
with nature, read, and write.

Simple living was also in full swing across the Atlantic. In
19th-century Paris, bohemian painters and writers like Henri
Murger—author of the autobiographical novel that was the basis for Puccini's opera *La Bohème*—valued artistic freedom over
a sensible and steady job, living off cheap coffee and conversation while their stomachs growled with hunger.

Redefining Luxury for the 21st Century

What all these people had in common was a desire to subordi-
nate their material desires to some other ideal—whether based
on ethics, religion, politics, or art. They believed that embracing
a life goal other than money could lead to a more meaningful
and fulfilling existence.

Woolman, for instance, "simplified his life in order to enjoy
the luxury of doing good," according to one of his biographers.
For Woolman, luxury was not sleeping on a soft mattress but
having the time and energy to work for social change, through
efforts such as the struggle against slavery.

Simple living is not about abandoning luxury, but discovering it in new places. These masters of simplicity are not just
telling us to be more frugal, but suggesting that we expand the
spaces in our lives where satisfaction does not depend on money.
Imagine drawing a picture of all those things that make your life
fulfilling, purposeful, and pleasurable. It might include friendships, family relationships, being in love, the best parts of your
job, visiting museums, political activism, crafting, playing sports,
volunteering, and people-watching.

There is a good chance that most of these activities cost very
little or nothing. We don't need to do much damage to our bank

balance to enjoy intimate friendships, uncontrollable laughter, dedication to causes or quiet time with ourselves.

As the humorist Art Buchwald put it, "The best things in life aren't things." The overriding lesson from Thoreau, Woolman, and other simple-living ancestors is that we should aim, year after year, to enlarge these areas of free and simple living on the map of our lives. That is how we will find the luxuries that constitute our hidden wealth.

CHAPTER 2

10 Things Science Says Will Make You Happy

Jen Angel

n recent years, psychologists and researchers have been dig-
ging up hard data on a question previously left to philosophers:
What makes us happy? Researchers like the father-son team Ed
Diener and Robert Biswas-Diener, Stanford psychologist Sonja
Lyubomirsky, and ethicist Stephen Post have studied people all
over the world to find out how things like money, attitude, culture, memory, health, altruism, and our day-to-day habits affect our well-being. The emerging field of positive psychology
is bursting with new findings that suggest your actions can have
a significant effect on your happiness and satisfaction with life.
Here are 10 scientifically proven strategies for getting happy.

1. **Savor Everyday Moments.** Pause now and then to smell a
   rose or watch children at play. Study participants who took
   time to "savor" ordinary events that they normally hurried
   through, or to think back on pleasant moments from their
   day, "showed significant increases in happiness and reduc-
   tions in depression," says psychologist Sonja Lyubomirsky[9]

2. **Avoid Comparisons.** While keeping up with the Joneses is
   part of American culture, comparing ourselves with others

can be damaging to happiness and self-esteem. Instead of comparing ourselves with others, focusing on our own personal achievement leads to greater satisfaction, according to Lyubomirsky.

3. **Put Money Low on the List.** People who put money high on their priority list are more at risk for depression, anxiety, and low self-esteem, according to researchers Tim Kasser and Richard Ryan. Their findings hold true across nations and cultures. "The more we seek satisfactions in material goods, the less we find them there," Ryan says. "The satisfaction has a short half-life—it's very fleeting." Money-seekers also score lower on tests of vitality and self-actualization.[10]

4. **Have Meaningful Goals.** "People who strive for something significant, whether it's learning a new craft or raising moral children, are far happier than those who don't have strong dreams or aspirations," say Ed Diener and Robert Biswas-Diener. "As humans, we actually require a sense of meaning to thrive."[11] Harvard's resident happiness professor, Tal Ben-Shahar, agrees: "Happiness lies at the intersection between pleasure and meaning. Whether at work or at home, the goal is to engage in activities that are both personally significant and enjoyable."[12]

5. **Take Initiative at Work.** How happy you are at work depends in part on how much initiative you take. Researcher Amy Wrzesniewski says that when we express creativity, help others, suggest improvements, or do additional tasks on the job, we make our work more rewarding and feel more in control.

6. **Make Friends, Treasure Family.** Happier people tend to have good families, friends, and supportive relationships, say Diener and Biswas-Diener. But it's not enough to be the life

of the party if you're surrounded by shallow acquaintances. "We don't just need relationships, we need close ones" that involve understanding and caring.[13]

7. **Smile Even When You Don't Feel Like It.** It sounds simple, but it works. "Happy people...see possibilities, opportunities, and success. When they think of the future, they are optimistic, and when they review the past, they tend to savor the high points," say Diener and Biswas-Diener. Even if you weren't born looking at the glass as half-full, with practice, a positive outlook can become a habit.

8. **Say Thank You Like You Mean It.** People who keep gratitude journals on a weekly basis are healthier, more optimistic, and more likely to make progress toward achieving personal goals, according to author Robert Emmons.[14] Research by Martin Seligman, founder of positive psychology, revealed that people who write "gratitude letters" to someone who made a difference in their lives score higher on happiness, and lower on depression—and the effect lasts for weeks.

9. **Get Out and Exercise.** A Duke University study shows that exercise may be just as effective as drugs in treating depression, without all the side effects and expense. Other research shows that in addition to health benefits, regular exercise offers a sense of accomplishment and opportunity for social interaction, releases feel-good endorphins, and boosts self-esteem.

10. **Give It Away Now!** Make altruism and giving part of your life, and be purposeful about it. Researcher Stephen Post says helping a neighbor, volunteering, or donating goods and services results in a "helper's high," and you get more health benefits than you would from exercise or quitting smoking.

Listening to a friend, passing on your skills, celebrating others' successes, and forgiveness also contribute to happiness, he says. Researcher Elizabeth Dunn found that those who spend money on others reported much greater happiness than those who spend it on themselves.[15]

CHAPTER 3

Who Pays the Price for Cheap Stuff?

Annie Leonard

'm a critic of consumerism, but I'm neither for nor against stuff. I confess that my T-shirt drawer is so full it's hard to close. (That's partly because I'm often given a Tee as a souvenir when I speak at a conference or event.) But of all the T-shirts I have accumulated over the years, there are only a few that I honestly care about. My favorite (no eye-rolling, please) is a green number from the Grateful Dead's 1982 New Year's Eve concert. To me this shirt, worn for more than 30 years by multiple members of my extended family, is both useful and beautiful, not only because I attended the concert but because a dear friend gave it to me, knowing how much I would treasure it. The label even says "Made in the USA," which makes me smile because so few things are made in this country anymore, as brands increasingly opt for low-paid workers in poor countries.

Our stuff should not be artifacts of indulgence and disposability, like toys that are forgotten 15 minutes after the wrapping comes off, but things that are both practical and meaningful. British philosopher William Morris said it best: "Have nothing in your house that you do not know to be useful or believe to be beautiful."

The life cycle of a simple cotton T-shirt—worldwide, 4 billion are made, sold, and discarded each year—knits together a chain of seemingly intractable problems, from the elusive definition of sustainable agriculture to the greed and classism of fashion marketing.[16]

The story of a T-shirt gives us insight into the complexity of our relationship with even the simplest stuff. It also demonstrates why consumer activism—boycotting or avoiding products that don't meet our personal standards for sustainability and fairness—will never be enough to bring about real and lasting change. Like a vast Venn diagram covering the entire planet, the environmental and social impacts of cheap T-shirts overlap and intersect on many layers, making it impossible to fix one without addressing the others.

Who Sews Those Tees?

And that takes me back to a day in 1990, in the slums of Port-au-Prince. I was in Haiti to meet with women who worked in sweatshops making T-shirts and other clothing for the Walt Disney Company. The women were nervous about speaking freely. We crowded into a tiny room inside a small cinderblock house. In sweltering heat, we had to keep the windows shuttered for fear that someone might see us talking. These women worked six days a week, eight hours a day, sewing clothes that they could never save enough to buy. Those lucky enough to be paid minimum wage earned about $15 a week.[17] The women described the grueling pressure at work, routine sexual harassment, and other unsafe and demeaning conditions.

They knew that Disney's CEO, Michael Eisner, made millions. A few years after my visit, a National Labor Committee documentary, *Mickey Mouse Goes to Haiti*, revealed that in 1996 Eisner made $8.7 million in salary plus $181 million in stock options—a staggering $101,000 an hour. The Haitian workers were paid one-half of 1 percent of the U.S. retail price of each garment they sewed.

The women wanted fair pay for a day's work—which in their dire straits meant $5 a day. They wanted to be safe, to be able to drink water when hot, and to be free from sexual harassment. They wanted to come home early enough to see their children before bedtime and to have enough food to feed them a solid meal when they woke. Their suffering, and the suffering of other garment workers worldwide, was a major reason the end product could be sold on the shelves of big-box retailers for a few dollars.

I asked them why they stayed in the teeming city, living in slums that had little electricity and no running water or sanitation, and working in such obviously unhealthy environments instead of returning to the countryside where they had grown up. They said the countryside simply couldn't sustain them anymore. Their families had given up farming, unable to compete against the rice imported from the U.S. and sold for less than half the price of the more labor-intensive, more nutritious native rice. It was all part of a plan, someone whispered, by the World Bank and U.S. Agency for International Development (USAID) to drive Haitians off their land and into the city to sew clothes for rich Americans. The destruction of farming as a livelihood was necessary to push people to the city, so people would be desperate enough to work all day in hellish sweatshops.

Their Proper Place

The next day I called on USAID. My jaw dropped as the man from the agency openly agreed with what at first had sounded like an exaggerated conspiracy theory. He said it wasn't efficient for Haitians to work on family farms to produce food that could be grown more cheaply elsewhere. Instead they should accept their place in the global economy—which, in his eyes, meant sewing clothes for us in the United States. But surely, I said, efficiency was not the only criterion. A farmer's connection to the land, healthy and dignified work, a parent's ability to spend time with his or her kids after school, a community staying intact generation after generation—didn't all these things have value?

"Well," he said, "if a Haitian really wants to farm, there is room for a handful of them to grow things like organic mangoes for the high-end export market." That's right: USAID's plan for the people of Haiti was not self-determination, but as a market for our surplus rice and a supplier of cheap seamstresses, with an occasional organic mango for sale at our gourmet grocery stores.

By 2008 Haiti was importing 80 percent of its rice. This left the world's poorest country at the mercy of the global rice market. Rising fuel costs, global drought, and the diversion of water to more lucrative crops—like the thirsty cotton that went into the Disney clothing—withered worldwide rice production. Global rice prices tripled over a few months, leaving thousands of Haitians unable to afford their staple food. *The New York Times* carried stories of Haitians forced to resort to eating mud pies made with sugar and oil.[18]

Citizens, Not Consumers

The problems of the T-shirt supply chain are just a smattering of the ills that not only result from the take-make-waste economy but make it possible. That's why striving to make responsible choices at the individual consumer level, while good, is just not enough. Change on the scale required by the severity of today's planetary and social crises requires a broader vision and a plan for addressing the root causes of the problem.

To do that we must stop thinking of ourselves primarily as consumers and start thinking and acting like citizens. That's because the most important decisions about stuff are not those made in the supermarket or department store aisles. They are the decisions made in the halls of government and business about what materials to use and what standards to uphold.

Consumerism, even when it tries to embrace "sustainable" products, is a set of values that teaches us to define ourselves, communicate our identity, and seek meaning through acquisition of stuff rather than through our values and activities and our community. Today we're so steeped in consumer culture that we head to the mall even when our houses and garages are full. We suffer angst over the adequacy of our belongings and amass crushing credit card debt to, as the author Dave Ramsey says, buy things we don't need with money we don't have, to impress people we don't like.

Citizenship, on the other hand, is about what Eric Liu, in *The Gardens of Democracy*, calls "how you show up in the world."[19] It's taking seriously our responsibility to work for broad, deep change that doesn't tinker around the margins of the system but achieves (forgive the activist-speak) a paradigm shift. Even "ethical consumerism" is generally limited to choosing the most responsible item on the menu, which often leaves us choosing between the lesser of two evils. Citizenship means working to change what's on the menu, and stuff that trashes the planet or harms people just doesn't belong. Citizenship means stepping beyond the comfort zones of everyday life and working with other committed citizens to make big, lasting change.

One of our best models of citizenship in the United States is the Civil Rights Movement of the 1960s. It's a myth that when Rosa Parks refused to move to the back of the bus it was a spontaneous act of individual conscience. She was part of a network of thousands of activists who mapped out their campaign, trained to be ready for the struggles to come, then put their bodies on the line in carefully planned civil disobedience. Consumer-based actions, such as boycotting segregated buses or lunch counters, were part of the campaign, but were done collectively and strategically. That model has been used, with varying degrees of success, in environmental, gay rights, pro-choice, and other movements. But consumer action alone—absent that larger citizen-led campaign—isn't enough to create deep change.

So yes, it is important to be conscious of our consumer decisions. But we're most powerful when this is connected to collective efforts for bigger structural change. As individuals, we can use less stuff if we remember to look inward and evaluate our well-being by our health, the strength of our friendships, and the richness of our hobbies and civic endeavors. And we can make even more progress by working together—as citizens, not consumers—to strengthen laws and business practices increasing efficiency and reducing waste.

As individuals, we can use less toxic stuff by prioritizing organic products, avoiding toxic additives, and ensuring safe recycling of our stuff. But we can achieve much more as citizens demanding tougher laws and cleaner production systems that protect public health overall. And there are many ways we can share more, like my community of several families does. Since we share our stuff, we only need one tall ladder, one pickup truck, and one set of power tools. This means we need to buy, own, and dispose of less stuff. From public tool lending libraries to online peer-to-peer sharing platforms, there are many avenues for scaling such efforts from the neighborhood to the national level.

We can't avoid buying and using stuff. But we can work to reclaim our relationship to it. We used to own our stuff; now our stuff owns us. But we can restore the proper balance.

CHAPTER 4

Why Everyone Is Happier in More Equitable Societies

Brooke Jarvis with Richard Wilkinson

For decades, British epidemiologist Richard Wilkinson has studied why some societies are healthier than others. In *The Spirit Level: Why Greater Equality Makes Societies Stronger* he and co-author Kate Pickett found that what the healthiest societies have in common is not that they have *more*—more income, more education, or more wealth—but that what they have is more equitably shared.[20]

Economic inequality has a host of corrosive impacts on whole societies, harming even those at the top of the pile. I sat down with Wilkinson to discuss the surprising importance of equality—and the best ways to build it.

Jarvis: You've studied the impact of inequality on public health for a long time. Did any of your recent findings surprise you?

Wilkinson: Oh, all of them. For many years, people working in public health have looked for a link between poverty and social problems like mental illness, crime, and infant mortality. We thought that once you found the relationship between income and death rates, for example, you should be able to predict what a state's death rate will be. Actually, though, that doesn't produce a good prediction. It turns out that what matters aren't the incomes themselves, but how unequal they are. If you're a more unequal state, the same level of income produces a higher death rate.

In less equal societies, we find perhaps eight times the number of teenage births per capita, 10 times the homicide rate, three times the rate of mental illness. We know from the findings that it's the status divisions themselves that create the problems. It's almost impossible to find any other consistent explanation.

Jarvis: How does thinking about these problems in terms of inequality rather than poverty change how we grapple with them?

Wilkinson: I think people have been worried by the scale of social problems in our societies—feeling that though we're materially very successful, a lot of stuff is going wrong, and we don't know why. The media are always full of these social problems, and they blame parents or teachers or lack of religion or whatever. It makes an important difference to people to have an analysis that really fits, not only in a sort of academic way. People have intuited for hundreds of years that inequality was divisive and socially corrosive.

Jarvis: Your findings related to crime and imprisonment rates seem to be particularly illustrative of the way inequality can lead to social corrosion.

Wilkinson: We quote a prison psychiatrist who spent 25 years talking to really violent men, and he says he has yet to see an act of violence which was not caused by people feeling disrespected, humiliated, or like they've lost face. Those are the triggers to violence, and they're more intense in more unequal societies, where status competition is intensified and we're more sensitive about social judgments.

Jarvis: When I first heard about your work, I expected it to deal with the material impacts of inequality. But your focus is different.

Wilkinson: Yes. This is about the psychosocial effects of inequality—the impact of living with anxiety about our feelings of superiority or inferiority. It's not the inferior housing that gives you heart disease, it's the stress, the hopelessness, the anxiety, the depression you feel around that.

Jarvis: What psychological impact does living in an unequal society have on people who are at the top?

Wilkinson: Status competition causes problems all the way up; we're all very sensitive to how we're judged. People spend thousands of pounds on a handbag with the right labels to make statements about themselves. In more unequal countries, people are more likely to get into debt. They work much longer hours—the most unequal countries work perhaps nine weeks longer in a year.

If you grow up in a consumerist society, you think of human beings as self-interested. It's not that we actually have an overwhelming desire to accumulate property, it's that we're concerned with how we're seen all the time. It's not material self-interest, it's that we experience ourselves through each other's eyes—and that's the reason for the labels and the clothes and the cars.

Jarvis: What's the effect of inequality on the way we perceive our communities—and how does that perception affect how they function?

Wilkinson: Inequality affects our ability to trust and our sense that we are part of a community. For instance, in more equal countries, two-thirds of the population may feel they can trust others in general, whereas in the more unequal countries or states, it may drop as low as 15 percent.

Inequality is a reflection of how strong hierarchies are, how much we share or how much we don't. It shows us which part of our potential we're developing. Have I got to fend for myself? Or is my survival dependent on good relationships? Are you going to steal from me? Or can we share?

Human beings can do both. We've lived in the most egalitarian and the most awful, hierarchical, tyrannical societies. It's very interesting that we can measure how unequal societies are and how that can elicit more of certain kinds of behavior.

Jarvis: Once we become aware of the impact of inequality on all of these social ills, what do we do about it?

Wilkinson: Countries seem to get greater equality in quite different ways. Sweden, for example, uses the big government way: There are very big differences in earnings, which are redistributed through taxes and benefits. It has a large welfare state. Japan, on the other hand, has smaller income differences to start with, does much less redistribution, and doesn't have such high social expenditure. But both countries do very well—they're among the more equal countries and their health and social outcomes are very good.

But we can't rely just on taxes and benefits to increase equality —the next government can undo them all at a stroke. We've got to get this structure of equality much more deeply embedded in our society. I think that means more economic democracy, or workplace democracy, of every kind. We're talking about friendly societies, mutual societies, employee ownership, employee representatives on the board, cooperatives—ways in which business is subjected to democratic influence. The bonus culture was only possible because the people at the top are not answerable to the employees at all.

Embedding greater equality and more democratic accountability in our institutions does much more than just changing income distribution or wealth distribution. This is about how we work better together.

Jarvis: Which is more important than ever, given that solving many of our major problems—climate change, for example—will require unprecedented levels of cooperation.

Wilkinson: Global warming, more than almost any other problem you can imagine, involves acting for the common good. It involves public spiritedness.

Inequality changes our perceptions—are you out for yourself, or do you recognize that we're in this together, that we've got to do these things for the common good?

And in more equal societies, where there's a stronger community life, less violence, and more trust, people give higher priority to the common good.

CHAPTER 5

We Are Hardwired to Cooperate and Share

Eric Michael Johnson

A century ago, industrialists like Andrew Carnegie believed that Darwin's theories justified an economy of vicious competition and inequality. They left us with an ideological legacy that says the corporate economy, in which wealth concentrates in the hands of a few, produces the best for humanity. This was always a distortion of Darwin's ideas. His 1871 book, *The Descent of Man,* argued that the human species had succeeded because of traits like sharing and compassion. "Those communities," he wrote, "which included the greatest number of the most sympathetic members would flourish best, and rear the greatest number of offspring."[21] Darwin was no economist, but wealth-sharing and cooperation have always looked more consistent with his observations about human survival than the elitism and hierarchy that dominates contemporary corporate life.

Nearly 150 years later, modern science has verified Darwin's early insights with direct implications for how we do business in our society. New peer-reviewed research by Michael Tomasello, an American psychologist and co-director of the Max Planck Institute for Evolutionary Anthropology in Leipzig, Germany, has synthesized three decades of research to develop a comprehensive evolutionary theory of human cooperation. What can we learn about sharing as a result?

Tomasello holds that there were two key steps that led to humans' unique form of interdependence. The first was all about who was coming to dinner. Approximately 2 million years ago, a fledgling species known as *Homo habilis* emerged on the great plains of Africa. At the same time that these four-foot-tall, bipedal apes appeared, a period of global cooling produced vast, open environments. This climate change event ultimately forced our hominid ancestors to adapt to a new way of life or perish entirely. Since they lacked the ability to take down large game, like the ferocious carnivores of the early Pleistocene, the solution they hit upon was scavenging the carcasses of recently killed large mammals. The analysis of fossil bones from this period has revealed evidence of stone-tool cut marks overlaid on top of carnivore teeth marks. The precursors of modern humans had a habit of arriving late to the feast.

However, this survival strategy brought an entirely new set of challenges: Individuals now had to coordinate their behaviors, work together, and learn how to share. For apes living in the dense rainforest, the search for ripe fruit and nuts was largely an individual activity. But on the plains, our ancestors needed to travel in groups to survive, and the act of scavenging from a single animal carcass forced proto-humans to learn to tolerate each other and allow each other a fair share. This resulted in a form of social selection that favored cooperation: "Individuals who attempted to hog all of the food at a scavenged carcass would be actively repelled by others," writes Tomasello, "and perhaps shunned in other ways as well."[22]

This evolutionary legacy can be seen in our behavior today, particularly among children who are too young to have been taught such notions of fairness. For example, in a 2011 study published in the journal *Nature*, anthropologist Katharina Hamann and her colleagues found that three-year-old children share food more equitably if they gain it through cooperative effort rather than via individual labor or no work at all.[23] In contrast, chimpanzees showed no difference in how they shared food under these different scenarios; they wouldn't necessarily hoard the food individually, but they placed no value on cooperative efforts either. The implication, according to Tomasello, is that human evolution has predisposed us to work collaboratively and given us an intuitive sense that cooperation deserves equal rewards.

The second step in Tomasello's theory leads directly into what kinds of businesses and economies are more in line with human evolution. Humans have, of course, uniquely large population sizes—much larger than those of other primates. It was the human penchant for cooperation that allowed groups to grow in number and eventually become tribal societies.

Humans, more than any other primate, developed psychological adaptations that allowed them to quickly recognize members of their own group (through unique behaviors, traditions, or forms of language) and develop a shared cultural identity in the pursuit of a common goal. "The result," says Tomasello, "was a new kind of interdependence and group-mindedness that went well beyond the joint intentionality of small-scale cooperation to a kind of collective intentionality at the level of the entire society."

CHAPTER 6

Why Saying Hello Matters

Akaya Windwood

One day a colleague and I were walking along the crowded waterfront in San Francisco. Coming toward us was a trio of young African-American men who were joking and playing. When we passed, I greeted them. Just as the last person walked by I heard him say, "Thanks for seeing us."

It took a minute for that to register. My companion said, "Did you hear what I heard?" It took me a moment before I could respond with, "Yes." My heart was breaking.

How could it be that I would be thanked for merely seeing someone? It took all of my self-control not to run back to those young men, gather them in my arms, and apologize for every person who had ever overlooked them, averted their eyes, or turned away. What must it be like to move through a world that refuses to meet one's eyes, that refuses to acknowledge one's very existence?

I could make an analysis and write this piece solely about the kind of pervasive racism which creates a very specific and limiting box in which African-American men are expected to live (and why they might feel invisible). Yet as I scan the world with those young men still in my heart, I notice that many kinds of people are often overlooked. The bag clerk at the grocery market, the person at the front desk, the folks who carry our mail or clean our streets or who are considered too old, or too young, or too…

What could happen if every day we were to greet each human as though they were worthy of notice and respect? What could happen if every day you were greeted as though you were worthy of notice and respect? What could change?

There is a certain cult of personality even among those of us whose lives are committed to social transformation. A lot of jockeying goes on around who gets noticed for acclaim, who gets the big dollars, who gets the media attention. Many of our social movements are less effective than they could be because of this competition for limelight or resources.

The reality is that most folks working for change do so because they care about their community or issue, not because they are looking for recognition or awards. Nonetheless, their work is crucial and necessary and is deserving of respect even if it goes unheralded. They may be unsung, but they are certainly heroes.

Everyone takes leadership in some way every day. Everyone. Most acts of leadership go unnoticed or unacknowledged, and that's a shame. The cultural pattern of noticing only some types of leadership and ignoring others contributes to the erasure of large groups of folks—women, poor and working-class people, and, yes, young African-American men.

If we can find ways to see each other, to honor the existence of every being who co-inhabits this wonderful earth with us—if no young person ever has need to thank a stranger for merely seeing them—then we will have done a fine thing.

Here's my invitation to you: let's take a month and intentionally notice those we would normally not see. Let's interrupt old patterns of not looking into the eyes of "those people" (whoever they are to you). Let's greet and acknowledge the folks we generally walk by or around and watch what happens.

The Practice of Happiness
(or, How You Can Get Some)

Christiania, Denmark (Photo by Birgit Carlsson)

Introduction

"Be happy for this moment. This moment is your life."

—Omar Khayyam, Persian poet, philosopher, and mathematician

What makes us happy? It's a perennial question and one much too important to be left to advertisers.

A starting point is to remember that we have choices. Viktor E. Frankl, concentration camp survivor and author of *Man's Search for Meaning,* wrote, "Forces beyond your control can take away everything you possess except one thing, your freedom to choose how you will respond to the situation."[1]

So we can choose to count our blessings or to count the slights and insults we endure during the day. We can seek out a vocation we love or grind our teeth and wait for retirement. And we can choose habits that enhance well-being by studying the art of mindfulness, kicking addictions, and taking time for exercise, healthy food, and good friends.

Sustainable happiness, in other words, is a habit of mind and a skill to be cultivated. One way to do this is through mindfulness, writes Matthieu Ricard, a Buddhist monk and author who serves as a translator for the Dalai Lama. Mindfulness—and its sibling, compassion—can lighten the burdens of our past and lessen our worries about the future. When we fully inhabit the moment, we become conscious of the interplay of our emotions and desires, and are more present with the people around us (see Chapter 7).

Mindfulness can also help those suffering from addictions, including both debilitating drug and alcohol problems and more subtle fixations—like the urge to have a digital device always at our fingertips. Dan Rollman decided to take a weekly tech Sabbath (see Chapter 8). And Dan Mahle found he was more loving with himself and a better friend and ally to women after he kicked his pornography habit (see Chapter 9).

Aristotle said, "Where the needs of the world and your talents cross, there lies your vocation." Author Roman Krznaric challenges us in Chapter 10 to take risks, experiment, and pursue the vocation we most want. That's what Shannon Hayes did when she gave up a nine-to-five career for an uncertain future on her family farm (Chapter 11). There are times when her family faces hard economic choices, she writes, but they get through them together with dignity and even joy.

Many say they have no time for happiness. Long work hours, mind-numbing commutes, and endless household responsibilities drain every waking moment. But making time to be with people you love boosts sustainable happiness. Family meals— prepared and served up in a way that invites everyone to linger— are worth the effort, Katherine Gustafson reports in Chapter 12. The benefits multiply as young people grow up in the embrace of family and stronger family bonds help kids and parents get through difficult times.

Regardless of how you live, practicing gratitude is almost certain to improve your outlook. Your grandmother might have told you to count your blessings. Today, we might keep a "gratitude journal," noting the things we appreciate over the course of a day. In Chapter 13, Jeremy Adam Smith calls gratitude a muscle—a tool, a lens, a paintbrush, a *choice*—that we apply to the many invisible blessings sustaining us each day.

CHAPTER 7

This Is Your Life—Show Up For It Mindfully

Matthieu Ricard

Happiness can't be reduced to a few agreeable sensations. Rather, it is a way of being and of experiencing the world —a profound fulfillment that suffuses every moment and endures despite inevitable setbacks.

The paths we take in search of happiness often lead us to frustration and suffering instead. We try to create outer conditions that we believe will make us happy. But it is the mind itself that translates outer conditions into happiness or suffering. This is why we can be deeply unhappy even though we "have it all"— wealth, power, health, a good family, etc.—and, conversely, we can remain strong and serene in the face of hardship.

Authentic happiness is a way of being and a skill to be cultivated. When we first begin, the mind is vulnerable and untamed, like that of a monkey or a restless child. It takes practice to gain inner peace, inner strength, altruistic love, forbearance, and other qualities that lead to authentic happiness.

His Holiness the Dalai Lama often teaches that, while there are limitations to how much information one can learn and to our physical performance, compassion can be developed boundlessly.

Practicing Happiness

It is not difficult to begin. You just have to sit from time to time, turn your mind within, and let your thoughts calm down. Focus your attention on a chosen object. It can be an object in your room, your breath, or your own mind. Inevitably, your mind will wander as you do this. Each time it does, gently bring it back to the object of concentration, like a butterfly that returns again and again to a flower.

In the freshness of the present moment, past is gone, future is not yet born, and—if one remains in pure mindfulness and freedom—disturbing thoughts arise and go without leaving a trace. That is basic meditation.

Pure consciousness without content is something all those who meditate regularly and seriously have experienced—it is not just some sort of Buddhist theory.

But meditation also means to cultivate basic human qualities, such as attention and compassion, and new ways of experiencing the world. What really matters is that a person gradually changes. Over months and years, we become less impatient, less prone to anger, less torn between hopes and fears. It becomes inconceivable to willingly harm another person. We develop a propensity toward altruistic behavior and the cluster of qualities that give us the resources to deal with the ups and downs of life.

Take the example of malevolent anger. Anger can fill our mental landscape and project its distorted reality on people and events. When we are overwhelmed by anger, we cannot dissociate from it. We perpetuate a vicious circle of affliction by re-kindling anger each time we see or remember the person who makes us angry. We become addicted to the cause of suffering.

But if we dissociate from anger and look at it with mindfulness, that which is aware of anger is not angry, and we can see that anger is just a bunch of thoughts. Anger doesn't cut like a knife, burn like a fire, or crush like a rock; it is nothing more than a product of our mind. Instead of "being" the anger, we understand that we are not the anger, in the same way that clouds are not the sky.

So, to deal with anger, we avoid letting our mind jump again and again to the trigger for our anger. Then we look at anger itself and keep our attention upon it. If we stop adding wood to a fire and just watch, the fire will die out. Likewise, anger will vanish away, without being forcibly repressed or allowed to explode.

There is no question of not experiencing emotions; it's a question of not being enslaved by them. Let emotions arise, but let them be freed from their afflictive components: distortion of reality, mental confusion, clinging, and suffering for oneself and others.

There is great virtue in resting from time to time in pure awareness of the present moment, and being able to refer to this state when afflictive emotions arise so that we do not identify with them and are not swayed by them.

It is difficult in the beginning, but becomes quite natural as you become increasingly familiar with such an approach. Whenever anger arises, you learn to recognize it right away. If you know someone to be a pickpocket, even if he mingles in a crowd, you will spot him right away and keep a careful eye on him.

Interdependence

Just as you can learn to deal with afflictive thoughts, you can learn to cultivate and enhance wholesome ones. To be filled with love and kindness is a win-win situation: you will enjoy lasting well-being for yourself, you'll act in altruistic ways towards others, and you'll be perceived as a good human being.

Acts of overflowing love, of pure, disinterested generosity—as when you make a child happy or help someone in need, even if nobody knows what you have done—generate a deep and heartwarming fulfillment.

Human qualities often come in clusters. Altruism, inner peace, strength, freedom, and genuine happiness thrive together like the parts of a nourishing fruit. Likewise, selfishness, animosity, and fear grow together. So, while helping others may not always be "pleasant," it leads the mind to a sense of inner peace, courage, and harmony with the interdependence of all things and beings.

Afflictive mental states, on the other hand, begin with self-centeredness, with an increase in the gap between self and others. These states are related to excessive self-importance and self-cherishing associated with fear or resentment toward others, and grasping for outer things as part of a hopeless pursuit of selfish happiness. A selfish pursuit of happiness is a lose-lose situation: you make yourself miserable and make others miserable as well.

Inner conflicts are often linked with excessive rumination on the past and anticipation of the future. You are not truly paying attention to the present moment, but are engrossed in your thoughts, going on and on in a vicious circle, feeding your ego and self-centeredness.

This is the opposite of bare attention. To turn your attention inside means to look at pure awareness itself and dwell without distraction, yet effortlessly, in the present moment.

If you cultivate these mental skills, after a while you won't need to apply contrived efforts anymore. You can deal with mental perturbations like the eagles I see from the window of my hermitage in the Himalayas deal with crows. The crows often attack them, diving at the eagles from above. But, instead of doing all kinds of acrobatics, the eagle simply retracts one wing at the last moment, lets the diving crow pass, and then extends its wing again. The whole thing requires minimal effort and causes little disturbance.

The Fragrance of Peace

When people experience "moments of grace," or "magical moments" in daily life, while walking in the snow under the stars or spending a beautiful moment with dear friends by the seaside, what is really happening? All of a sudden, they have left their burden of inner conflicts behind. They feel in harmony with others, with themselves, with the world. It is wonderful to fully enjoy such magical moments, but it is also revealing to understand why they feel so good: pacification of inner conflicts; a better sense of interdependence with everything rather than fragmenting reality; and a respite from the mental toxins of aggression and obsession. This will lead not just to a few moments of grace but to a lasting state of well-being that we may call genuine happiness.

In this state, feelings of insecurity gradually give way to a deep confidence that you can deal with life's ups and downs. Your equanimity will spare you from being swayed like mountain grass in the wind by every possible praise and blame, gain and loss, comfort and discomfort. You can always draw on deep inner peace, and the waves at the surface will not appear as threatening.

CHAPTER 8

Give Yourself a Break: Take a Tech Sabbath

Erika Kosina

Dan Rollman recently noticed a disturbing trend in his social interactions: "I was starting to get more birthday wishes on my Facebook wall than phone calls and handwritten cards from family and friends."

This inspired him to create the Sabbath Manifesto, which encourages people to enjoy time with loved ones, silence, the outdoors, and other pleasures they may remember from the time before the Internet took over every free moment.

"I just want to spark some dialogue about the pace of life and our relationship with technology," he said.

Across the country, Americans are starting to think about how a constant stream of electronic communication affects the quality of our lives. Many of us are consciously unplugging every once in a while, and encouraging others to do the same.

Sal Bednarz made headlines in San Francisco when he asked customers in his café to turn off their laptops for a day. Bednarz first opened the Actual Café in his North Oakland neighborhood to increase social interaction among neighbors, but he found that the Internet got in the way.

"When you walk into a café where there are 20 people and they are all on laptops and nobody is talking to each other, it creates a certain experience," he said. "Unless you experience a café environment where there are no laptops, you don't know what you are missing."

The Actual Café is now laptop-free every weekend. Bednarz isn't anti-laptop per se, but he recognizes that people need real connection—not just on screens. "That's where the name of the café came from: actual interaction," he said.

One day, local businesses in San Francisco sponsored a Tech-Free Day, inviting participants to visit an unplugged café or attend a potluck picnic. Aubrey Harmon, a self-described "multitasking stay-at-home mom who also writes," unplugged her TV, computer, and smart phone and went to the picnic—which banned technology but encouraged singing along with a band that played an acoustic set.

Harmon found she was more present at the picnic when not hiding behind a camera or phone and decided to make breaks from technology part of her family life: "I realized that it's good for my son to balance TV and technology with face-to-face and outdoor time."

The Sabbath Manifesto offers ten principles for observing a weekly day of rest from technology. Rollman developed it in collaboration with Reboot, a nonprofit organization working to make traditional Jewish rituals relevant in modern life (though, the creators say, you don't have to be religious for a tech Sabbath to be relevant).

Tech-Free Day and related events like the National Day of Unplugging are resonating deeply across the United States. Bednarz is thrilled that his café's laptop-free weekends are building actual community.

The Sabbath Manifesto —10 Ways to Take a Day Off

1. Avoid technology	**6.** Light candles
2. Connect with loved ones	**7.** Drink wine
3. Nurture your health	**8.** Eat bread
4. Get outside	**9.** Find silence
5. Avoid commerce	**10.** Give back

He remembers a neighborhood filmmaker who was working in his café during the week, but still being mindful of the unplugged philosophy. "She made a point of taking breaks and talking to people next to her," he said "She came up to me afterward and thanked me because she had made two new friends, and five new business contacts."

"It goes back to Thoreau and living deliberately instead of mindlessly," says Frank Bures, a Minneapolis-based travel writer who decided to make his Mondays Internet-free. "How do you want to spend your life? Staring at a screen and following link trails, or being in your own mind?"

Bures believes the ability to focus our attention on a single problem for a long time is endangered by the constant interruptions of electronic communications. To him, this is tragic: "Your attention is finite, and it is what defines your life. If you just give it away, your life adds up to nothing."

CHAPTER 9

Kick Your Addictions, Return to Intimacy

Dan Mahle

I remember when I first discovered Internet porn. I was 17 years old. Fascinated by this world of unleashed sexual expression and fantasy, I couldn't get enough of it. As I grew up and began exploring my own sexuality, I discovered just how different watching pixels on a screen was compared to the intimacy of making love with another human being. I thought I'd outgrow my porn habit over time. But I didn't.

Porn had become an addiction. And, like most addicts, I was ashamed to talk about it or even admit it was a problem.

"Everybody watches porn," I remember hearing. It seemed so pervasive and culturally accepted that having an actual conversation about it was a total non-starter. So I kept it to myself.

I didn't realize how much watching porn had manipulated my mind, warping my sexuality, numbing my feelings, and affecting my relationships with women. And I was not alone.

According to a recent study, more than 70 percent of 18- to 34-year-old men visit porn sites in a typical month.[2] And it's not just guys watching sex online. It is estimated that one in three porn users today are women.[3]

To me, what is worrying about porn is not how many people use it, but how many people *have found themselves addicted to it.*[4]

Impacts of Porn

Numerous studies have linked porn viewership and increased instances of sexism and violence. This includes an obsession with looking at women rather than interacting with them (voyeurism) and the trivialization of rape and widespread acceptance of rape culture—an acceptance that is fueled by depictions of women in porn videos pretending to desire violent and abusive sexual acts.

Watching too much porn can also cause erectile dysfunction, inability to orgasm when not watching porn, detachment from your physical body, emotional unavailability and numbness, lack of focus and patience, poor memory, and general lack of interest in reality.[5]

Watching porn contributes to many men's inability to relate to women in an honest and intimate way despite a longing to feel loved and connected.

Why I Quit Watching

I always felt like a hypocrite watching porn. Here I was, a man who is striving to be an ally to women, perpetuating the very culture of violence and misogyny that I was ostensibly trying to fight. The reality was that most of the videos I found online had titles that included words like "bitch" or "slut" and showcased controlling behaviors that were rooted in a culture where women are nothing more than sexual bodies to be exploited and dominated by men.

When I am deeply honest, I have to admit I was both intrigued and disgusted by these images. By that time, my mind had been trained to find aggressive, misogynistic, and even nonconsensual sex arousing. It is difficult for me to admit, but it got to a point where I felt physically ill watching the videos, and yet I kept watching. That's when I realized I was dealing with an addiction.

So after a decade of use, I decided to quit watching porn for one year, both to see if I could and to find out how life might be different.

A year later, here are some of the things I've gained.

Life after Porn

Since dropping porn, I have restored a sense of personal integrity that had been missing from my life. Regaining this integrity has allowed me to move through a lot of my shame and find myself in a new space of deepening love for myself and others. I've also noticed that I am often able to stay more present with women now, rather than projecting fantasies onto them. This was hard to do when my mind was cluttered with images from porn videos. This newfound presence has also allowed me to begin to dismantle some of the subconscious sexism within myself, helping me work toward becoming a better friend to the women in my life.

I've expanded my sense of self by learning how to move out of my head and into my heart. After many long years void of emotional expression, I've reconnected to my tears. This release of suppressed emotional tension has unlocked a lot of joy in my life. All of this has helped me begin to shift my sexuality from physical detachment to true intimacy, presence, and embodiment.

I've become much more willing to let go of control, to improvise, and to accept people's differences. I trust myself more than I ever have and, as a result, my sense of self-confidence has soared. I wake up every morning grateful to be alive, clear about my life's purpose, and passionate about the work I am doing in the world. My life today has a depth of authenticity and power that I never felt before.

Stepping Up

As the Franciscan priest and compassion advocate Richard Rohr has written, "pain that is not transformed is transmitted."[6] And this pain is often transmitted in the form of violence. So how do we, as men, break this cycle? It's clear to me that we will never transform our pain within a culture of silence. It is only by bringing our shadows to the light that we can diffuse the power they hold over us.

I am committed to a world of love, respect, and safety for all people. I'm sick of all the shame, numbness, and secrecy surrounding porn and addiction. I'm saddened to hear about all the guilt people feel (from churches, parents, teachers, etc.) simply for wanting to express their sexuality in healthy and authentic ways. And I'm outraged by the violence, degradation, and exploitation of women. Enough is enough. A culture of love and healing can only be built on a foundation of radical honesty and integrity, built from the ground up in our own lives.

CHAPTER 10

Stop Worrying and Find Work You Love

Roman Krznaric

The idea of fulfilling work—a job that reflects our passions, talents, and values—is a modern invention. Open Dr. Johnson's celebrated *Dictionary*, published in 1755, and the word "fulfillment" doesn't even appear. But today our expectations are higher, which helps explain why job satisfaction has declined to a record low of 47 percent in the U.S., and is even lower in Europe.[7]

If you count yourself amongst those who are unhappy in their jobs, or at least have that occasional niggling feeling that your work and self are out of alignment, how are you supposed to go about finding a meaningful career? What does it take to overcome the fear of change and negotiate the labyrinth of choices, especially in tough economic times?

Confusion is Perfectly Normal

First, a consoling thought: being confused about career choice is perfectly normal and utterly understandable. In the pre-industrial period there were around 30 standard trades—you might decide to be a blacksmith or a barrel-maker—but now career websites list more than 12,000 different jobs. The result? We can become so anxious about making the wrong choice that we end up making no choice at all, staying in jobs that we grew out of long ago. Psychologist Barry Schwartz calls this the "paradox of choice": too many options can lead to decision paralysis, and we are like deer caught in the headlights.[8]

Then add to this our built-in aversion to risk. Human beings tend to exaggerate everything that could possibly go wrong, or as Nobel Prize-winning psychologist Daniel Kahneman says, "We hate losing twice as much as we love winning," whether at the casino table or when making career choices.[9] So our brains are not well calibrated for daring to change profession. We need to recognize that confusion is natural, and get ready to move beyond it.

Aim To Be a Wide Achiever, Not a High Achiever

For more than a century, Western culture has been telling us that the best way to use our talents and be successful is to specialize and become a high achiever, an expert in a narrow field—say a corporate tax accountant or an anesthesiologist.

But an increasing number of people feel that this approach fails to cultivate the many sides of who they are. For them, it makes more sense to embrace the idea of being a "wide achiever" rather than a high achiever. Take inspiration from Renaissance generalists like Leonardo da Vinci, who would paint one day, then do some mechanical engineering, followed by a few anatomy experiments on the weekend.

Today this is called being a "portfolio worker," doing several jobs simultaneously and often freelance. Management thinker Charles Handy says this is not just a good way of spreading risk in an insecure job market, but is an extraordinary opportunity made possible by the rise of opportunities for flexible work: "For the first time in the human experience, we have a chance to shape our work to suit the way we live instead of our lives to fit our work. We would be mad to miss the chance."[10]

Ask yourself this: What would being a wide achiever encompass for me?

Find Where Your Values and Talents Meet

The wisest single piece of career advice was proffered 2,500 years ago when Aristotle declared, "Where the needs of the world and your talents cross, there lies your vocation." And he would surely endorse contemporary research findings showing that those pursuing money and status are unlikely to feel fulfilled: the Mercer Global Engagement Scale places "base pay" as only number seven out of 12 factors predicting job satisfaction.[11]

The best alternative, says Harvard's Howard Gardner, is to find an ethical career, focused on values and issues that matter to you and that also allows you to do what you're really good at.[12] That might sound like a luxury when there are long lines at job centers. But consider that in the 34 countries of the Organization for Economic Co-Operation and Development, the social enterprise sector, in which organizations strive not only to make profits but also to improve social and environmental conditions, is growing 250 percent faster than the rest of the economy.[13]

So imagine yourself in three parallel universes. In each of them, you can spend next year trying a job in which your talents meet the needs of the world. What three jobs would you be excited to try?

Act First, Reflect Later

The biggest mistake people make when changing careers is to follow the traditional "plan then implement" model. You draw up lists of personal strengths, weaknesses, and ambitions, then match your profile to particular professions; at that point you start sending out applications. But there's a problem: It typically doesn't work. You might find a new job, but despite your expectations it is unlikely to be fulfilling.

Instead of thinking and then acting, we should act first and reflect later by trying out jobs in the real world—by shadowing, interning, or volunteering, testing out careers through experiential learning. Laura van Bouchout gave herself the thirtieth birthday present of spending a whole year trying 30 different jobs—a kind of "radical sabbatical." She was manager of a cat hotel, then shadowed a member of the European Parliament, and found that working in advertising was unexpectedly exhilarating.

Challenge yourself: What is your first branching project going to be? And what is the very first step you can take towards making it happen?

Discover a Little Madness

Changing careers is a frightening prospect: Of those who want to leave their jobs, around half are too afraid to take the plunge.[14] Ultimately, there is no avoiding the fact that it is a risk.

Ask successful career changers how to overcome the fear and most say the same thing: In the end you have to stop thinking and just do it. That may be why nearly all cultures have recognized that to live a meaningful and vibrant life, we need to take some chances—or else we might end up looking back on our lives with regret.

"Carpe diem," advised the Roman poet Horace: seize the day before it is too late. "If not now, when?" asked the rabbinical sage Hillel the Elder. Personally, I like the way *Zorba the Greek* puts it: "A man needs a little madness, or else he never dares to cut the rope and be free."

It is only by treating our working lives as an ongoing experiment that we will be able to find a job that is big enough for our spirits.

CHAPTER 11

Follow Your Calling—Even When It Scares You

Shannon Hayes

It should have been a high point in my life. I had just successfully defended my dissertation and had three potential job opportunities. But I found myself pacing around our cabin or walking the hills of my family's farm, alternately weeping and hurling invectives into the country air. Bob and I were fighting with a force I'd never seen.

The simple fact was, I didn't want the job I'd spent years working toward.

"I thought you wanted this! Why the hell did you just spend the last four years at Cornell? Why did we just go through with this? Why did you say that's what you wanted?"

What could I tell him? Because I didn't know any other way to stay close to my family's land and make the kind of money I thought we needed? Because I didn't believe there was a future in farming? Because the only way I thought I could manifest my talents was within an institution that would offer me a paycheck?

"What do you want?"

"To write and farm."

"Then do it."

"We need money. I don't know how to do it."

But I did know how. Since our arrival on these shores, every generation of my family has farmed. I was in the first generation that didn't believe we could make a living doing it. Our neighbors lived, laughed, and loved on these rocky hillsides, and they did it with four-figure incomes. And yet, I'd come to believe that, on these same hills, we needed six. Somewhere along the line, I had stopped believing the evidence that was before me and started believing one of the central myths of modern American culture: that a family requires a pile of money just to survive in some sort of comfort and that "his and her" dual careers were an improvement over times past.

What had changed? Why did I believe we needed so much? It was a puzzle to me at the time. In retrospect I see that my generation grew up immersed in media that equated affluence with respect, happiness, and fulfillment. We heard a national dialogue that predicted the end of the family farm. Those messages shook our security in our lifestyle—we ended up questioning our own experience.

After all, I grew up working on my neighbor's farm. We had fantastic midday feasts, the house was warm in the winter, and there was always a little spare cash on hand to donate when someone was in trouble. And plenty of pies got baked, gratis, to contribute to the local church bake sale and turkey supper. I was in my mid-20s before I discovered just how little money they lived on.

That was how many people lived as I was growing up in West Fulton, New York, where my family still farms. The steep hillsides and frosty valleys render most modern industrial farming technologies impractical in my community. Cash crops are few. To survive, my neighbors had to produce as many of the things they needed as possible and buy only the things they absolutely couldn't make or grow at home. They grew and preserved food, sewed and mended clothes, and did their own repairs, improvements, and upkeep on the farm.

Ultimately, Bob and I joined my parents in the grassfed meat business, where we now work, like many others, to help build a local, sustainable food system that enables us to make an adequate living. Keeping the lessons of our neighbors in mind, we determined that the key to survival was producing as much as we could and buying only what we must. We raise and sell meat for our income, but we also render fat into soap, preserve the summer harvest for winter, and spend more time socializing with friends and neighbors at home for entertainment than we do going out and spending money on amusements. Even with two children, we live very well on a bit more than $40,000 per year, a far cry from the six-figure income that I once thought we needed.

Bob and I are fortunate in having access to my parents' land and to the knowledge that they and other farmers in the area share with us. That has made our transition easier. But it doesn't take a farm to begin the journey. Americans from different walks of life all around the country are taking steps in their own households, whether they are rural, urban, or suburban. Even without a land base, they are finding ways to turn their homes from units of consumption to units of production. They are walking and biking, rather than driving; cooking rather than going out for fast food; playing music and creating art rather than buying entertainment from mass media; preserving the harvest from local farms rather than buying packaged foods from an industrialized food system; brewing beer in the corner of their apartments; learning how to fix their own toilets and cars; repairing their clothing or finding ways to repurpose it; networking with neighbors to barter for goods and services that they cannot produce.

The upshot is a growing movement of Americans who are creating a new home economics where there is time for family members to enjoy each other, where the ecological footprint is greatly reduced, and where, instead of the family working to support the household, the household works to support the family. With this new home economy, relationships are deeper, children are more connected with the life systems that support them, and the family can make it through economic hard times with dignity and joy.

CHAPTER 12

Share Meals with Loved Ones

Katherine Gustafson

When the 10 Garcia-Prats boys got together every night for dinner, they shared more than food around the table. They talked about the successes and frustrations of their days. The older boys helped the younger ones cut their meat. They compared their picks for the World Cup, a conversation that turned into an impromptu geography lesson.

Their mother, Cathy, author of *Good Families Don't Just Happen: What We Learned from Raising Our Ten Sons and How It Can Work for You*, strove to make the dinner table warm and welcoming, a place where her boys would want to linger.[15] "Our philosophy is that dinnertime is not just a time to feed your body; it's a time to feed your mind and your soul," she told me over the phone from her Houston, Texas, home. "It lets us have an opportunity to share our day, be part of each others' lives."

Today, families like the Garcia-Prats are the exception. According to the 2011–2012 National Survey of Children's Health, fewer than half of Americans eat meals daily with their families, a statistic that highlights the breakneck pace at which we live and our grab-and-go food culture.[16] Increasing economic pressures only exacerbate these cultural trends, as many families are forced to work two jobs to afford the basics and have little time to slow down and have dinner.

But the deterioration of the family meal may be more damaging than we realize. "Our lives have gotten so hectic and so busy that if you don't set aside time as a family, I think you just get lost," said Garcia-Prats. "Then you're just individuals living in a building, instead of a family living in a home, supporting each other and being there for each other."

Dinner and Happiness

When food advocate and chef Tom French asked a student how she felt after his organization, the Experience Food Project, began replacing the bland, processed food in her school cafeteria with fresh, healthy school lunches, he received an unexpected answer.

"She gave it some serious thought," he told me over the phone. "Then she said, 'you know, I feel respected.'"

Moments like this make French believe that adults who prepare quality meals for children are offering something more important than a nutrition lesson: They are communicating that they care. This is why the Experience Food Project teaches PTA parents about the importance of prioritizing family meals and helps them schedule the logistics of dinnertime.

French says there are "mountains of statistical data" correlating family dinner with benefits such as better communication, higher academic performance, and improved eating habits. Having dinner together boosts family cohesiveness and is associated with children's motivation in school, positive outlook, and avoidance of high-risk behaviors. Teens who frequently eat with their families are half as likely to smoke or use pot than those who rarely have family dinners, according to researchers at The National Center on Addiction and Substance Abuse at Columbia University (CASA).[17]

The correlation between family dinner and well-adjusted teens is so strong that CASA launched the first annual Family Day, an event honoring the family meal. The day recognizes that "parental engagement fostered during frequent family dinners is an effective tool to help keep America's kids substance free."

President Obama officially proclaimed Family Day 2010, noting that it served as an opportunity to "recommit to creating a solid foundation for the future health and happiness of all our nation's children."[18]

Communities from all over the country held Family Day celebrations, and some made the event into a week-long affair. Families found creative ways to celebrate each others' company over food—putting together homemade pizzas, picnicking, doing activities from CASA's Family Dinner Kit, and eating at restaurants offering discounts for the occasion.

Such events draw attention to the ways in which meals together help families strengthen their relationships, according to Joseph A. Califano Jr., CASA founder and chairman and former U.S. Secretary of Health, Education, and Welfare. "The more often teens have dinner with their parents, the more likely they are to report talking to their parents about what's going on in their lives," said Califano in a statement to press. "In today's busy and overscheduled world, taking the time to come together for dinner really makes a difference in a child's life."[19]

Family dinner also encourages the development of language skills and emotional intelligence in children.[20] During dinner conversations, children learn how to articulate their feelings and experiences and to communicate respect—whether that means asking politely for a dish or talking about their day at school. Research shows that children who have acquired skills in identifying and expressing emotion and negotiating conflict often experience less distress, have fewer behavior problems, hold more positive attitudes about school, and exhibit better academic performance.[21]

Fusion Cuisine

Finding ways to connect is increasingly important as families become more diverse and must negotiate cultural and generational difference. "People are tired and they are working and they are blending cultures and blending generations," said French, who grew up in a household with his great-grandmother.

Families of all types benefit from sharing life's daily ups and downs around the table. In a 2010 study of a group of racially diverse, low-income, urban youth, kids who ate family dinner more frequently had more positive perceptions of their communication with their parents.[22] Extended and blended families may find that dinner solidifies fledgling or fragile bonds. And families that unite multiple cultures can make the sharing of specific traditions and dishes—which, as French puts it, "carry generations of cultural DNA"—into a centerpiece of family bonding.

As Garcia-Prats sees it, dinner is a time when families can celebrate their differences. "We learn diversity appreciation in our homes," she said. "It's going to be hard to appreciate someone else's religion or ethnicity or culture if we haven't even learned to appreciate the uniqueness of each person in our own family. It's one of our philosophies: We are 12 unique individuals in this home."

At dinner, we bridge the gaps between us by sharing our food and the stories of our lives. And the moments we spend together at the table form the basis of something remarkably profound. Call it what you will—sibling bonding, communicating respect, bridging cultures—but at the very least it is, as Garcia-Prats told me, "not just about food." It is about the way food can connect us.

CHAPTER 13

Choose Gratitude

Jeremy Adam Smith

'm terrible at gratitude.

How bad am I? I'm so bad at gratitude that most days, I don't notice the sunlight on the leaves of the Berkeley oaks as I ride my bike down the street. I forget to be thankful for the guy who hand-brews that delicious cup of coffee I drink midway through every weekday morning. I don't even know the dude's name.

I usually take for granted that I have legs to walk on, eyes to see with, arms I can use to hug my son. I forget my son! I generally remember to pick him up from school and feed him dinner. But I forget all the time how much he's changed my life for the better.

Gratitude is the mental tool we use to remind ourselves of the good stuff. It's a lens that helps us to see the things that don't make it onto our lists of problems to be solved. It's a bright red paintbrush we apply to otherwise-invisible blessings, like clean streets or health or enough food to eat.

Gratitude doesn't erase problems and threats. We can lose jobs, we can be attacked on the street, and we can get sick. I've experienced all of those things. I remember those harrowing times at unexpected moments: My heart beats faster, my throat constricts. That's when I need to turn on the gratitude.

If I do that enough, the psychological research suggests my gratitude might just become a habit.[23] I could increase my chances of psychologically surviving hard times[24] and stand a chance to be happier in the good times.

Here's what truly grateful people do.

Once in a While, They Think About Death and Loss.

Contemplating endings makes you more grateful for the life you currently have, according to several studies.

When Araceli Friasa and colleagues asked people to visualize their own deaths, their gratitude measurably increased.[25] Similarly, when Minkyung Koo and colleagues asked people to envision the sudden disappearance of their romantic partners from their lives, they became more grateful to their partners.[26] The same goes for imagining that some positive event, like a job promotion, never happened.

This isn't just theoretical: When you find yourself taking a good thing for granted, try giving it up for a little while.[27] Researchers Jordi Quoidbach and Elizabeth Dunn had 55 people eat a piece of chocolate—and then the researchers told some of those people to resist chocolate for a week and others to binge on chocolate if they wanted. They left a third group to their own devices.

Guess who ended up happiest, according to self-reports? The people who abstained from chocolate. And who were the least happy? The people who binged.

They Take the Time to Smell the Roses.

And they also smell the coffee, the bread baking in the oven, the aroma of a new car—whatever gives them pleasure.

Loyola University psychologist Fred Bryant finds that savoring positive experiences makes them stick in your brain and increases their benefits to your psyche—and the key, he argues, is expressing gratitude for the experience. That's one of the ways appreciation and gratitude go hand in hand.[28]

You might also consider adding some little ritual to how you experience the pleasures of the body: A study published in *Psychological Science* finds that rituals like prayer or even just shaking a sugar packet "make people pay more attention to food, and paying attention makes food taste better," as Emily Nauman reported in *Greater Good,* the online magazine of the Greater Good Science Center (GGSC) at UC Berkeley.[29]

They Take the Good Things as Gifts, Not Birthrights.

What's the opposite of gratitude? Entitlement—the attitude that people owe you something just because you're so very special.

"In all its manifestations, a preoccupation with the self can cause us to forget our benefits and our benefactors or to feel that we are owed things from others and therefore have no reason to feel thankful," writes Robert Emmons, co-director of the GGSC's Expanding Gratitude project. "Counting blessings will be ineffective because grievances will always outnumber gifts."[30]

The antidote to entitlement, argues Emmons, is to see that we did not create ourselves—we were created, if not by evolution, then by God; or if not by God, then by our parents. Likewise, we are never truly self-sufficient. Humans need other people to grow our food and heal our injuries; we need love, and for that we need family, partners, friends, and pets.

"Seeing with grateful eyes requires that we see the web of interconnection in which we alternate between being givers and receivers," writes Emmons. "The humble person says that life is a gift to be grateful for, not a right to be claimed."[31]

They're Grateful to People, Not Just Things.

"Experiences that heighten meaningful connections with others —like noticing how another person has helped you, acknowledging the effort it took, and savoring how you benefited from it—engage biological systems for trust and affection, alongside circuits for pleasure and reward," writes GGSC science director Emiliana Simon-Thomas.

So saying thanks to my son might make him happier and it can strengthen our emotional bond. Thanking the guy who makes my coffee can deepen our understanding of interconnectedness.

They Mention the Pancakes.

Grateful people are habitually specific. They don't say, "I love you because you're just so wonderfully wonderful, you!" Instead, the really skilled grateful person will say: "I love you for the pancakes you make when you see I'm hungry and the way you massage my feet after work even when you're really tired and how you give me hugs when I'm sad so that I'll feel better."

The reason for this is pretty simple: It makes the expression of gratitude feel more authentic because it reveals that the thanker was genuinely paying attention and isn't just going through the motions. The richest thank you's will acknowledge intentions and costs and describe the value of benefits received.

When Amie Gordon and colleagues studied gratitude in couples, they found that spouses signal grateful feelings through more caring and attentive behavior. They ask clarifying questions; they respond to trouble with hugs and to good news with smiles. "These gestures," Gordon writes, "can have profound effects: Participants who were better listeners during those conversations in the lab had partners who reported feeling more appreciated by them."[32]

They *Thank* **Outside the Box.**

Let's get real: Pancakes, massages, hugs? Boring! Most of these examples are easy.

But here's who the really tough-minded grateful person thanks: the boyfriend who dumped her, the homeless person who asked for change, the boss who laid him off.

We're graduating from Basic to Advanced Gratitude, so pay attention. And since I am still working on Basic, I'll turn once again to Dr. Emmons for guidance: "It's easy to feel grateful for the good things. No one 'feels' grateful that he or she has lost a job or a home or good health or has taken a devastating hit on his or her retirement portfolio."

In such moments, he says, gratitude becomes a critical cognitive process—a way of thinking about the world that can help us turn disaster into a stepping stone. If we're willing and able to look, he argues, we can find a reason to feel grateful even to people who have harmed us. We can thank that boyfriend for being brave enough to end a relationship that wasn't working; the homeless person for reminding us of our advantages and vulnerability; the boss for forcing us to face new challenges.

Processing experiences through the gratitude lens doesn't mean masking pain with "superficial happiology."

"Instead, it means realizing the power you have to transform an obstacle into an opportunity," Emmons writes. "It means reframing a loss into a potential gain, recasting negativity into positive channels for gratitude."

PART THREE

Sustainable Happiness and the Beloved Community

Occupy Wichita, Kansas (Photo by Matthew Katzenberger)

Introduction

Martin Luther King Jr. spoke often of a "Beloved Community"—a vision of a society in which there is no poverty, hunger, racism, or war. Instead, love, sharing, trust, peace, and justice prevail. "It is this type of understanding goodwill that will transform the deep gloom of the old age into the exuberant gladness of the new age," King said in a 1956 speech entitled "Facing the Challenge of a New Age." "It is this love which will bring about miracles in the hearts of men."[1]

This vision serves as inspiration for Hawaiian native activist, Zen priest, and community facilitator Puanani Burgess, who has developed a group process she calls "Building the Beloved Community." She asks, "What if we were truly able to see and honor the gifts each of us offers?" (See Chapter 14).

Fania Davis, head of Restorative Justice for Oakland Youth, has devoted herself to honoring the worth and dignity of each of the students she works with in the Oakland, California, school system, as she describes in Chapter 15. By using the healing approach of restorative justice instead of harsh punishment, she helps break the cycles of poverty and pain that feed the school-to-prison pipeline, offering urban youth a chance at sustainable happiness.

Building community starts close to home. Authors John McKnight and Peter Block describe the fabric of neighborliness that is woven when people in a neighborhood with skills to share are matched up with those who want to learn (see Chapter 16).

Neighborhoods that draw people out of their homes and into common spaces build relationships, trust, and community well-being. In Chapter 17, Jay Walljasper, senior fellow at On the Commons, shows how cooperative housing, shared backyards, and tiny parks enhance neighborliness.

In Chapter 18, filmmaker Pavithra Mehta tells the story of a pay-it-forward restaurant that offers food for free—you are invited to pay for the next person's meal. Acts of kindness delight and elicit yet more generosity, and sustainable happiness ensues.

Our beloved community isn't complete, though, unless we include the natural world. Internationally renowned scientist, author, and activist Vandana Shiva calls for a recognition of the rights of all the species that are part of the web of life. "The forest ... teaches us enoughness: as a principle of equity, how to enjoy the gifts of nature without exploitation and accumulation," she says in Chapter 19. "The end of consumerism and accumulation is the beginning of the joy of living."

From your neighborhood to your neighboring ecosystem, sustainable happiness means joining fully in this Beloved Community of all life.

CHAPTER 14

The Story of Your Gift

Puanani Burgess

I am a facilitator and mediator, and I use a process I call "Building the Beloved Community" to help people talk to each other. I arrived at this process after years working as an activist for the rights of my people, the Hawaiian people. After becoming a Zen priest, I realized that all people are my people and that I had the responsibility to care for all of them.

With this process, I help people go to the deepest places, below the *piko* (belly button) into their *naʻau* (guts). We do this as part of a ceremony, a sacred process that helps to level the playing field. It's a safe space where we can all see each other as human, where we develop curiosity about each other, and where conflict can be transformed. It's a process I've used with incarcerated women and among government officials and community advocates trying to find common ground.

In this process, I ask people to tell three stories.

The first is the story of all of your names—not just the ones you use during short introductions. When you speak of your names, you tell the story of your family, your people, and your history. And you share your feelings about your name— who named you, what your name means.

The second is the story of your community, however you define it. Who makes up the group that you relate to?

The third story I ask is the most difficult for many people; it is the story of your gift. This is not the story of your skills, experiences, degrees, or titles. It's difficult because talking about your gifts can seem like bragging, which makes many people uncomfortable.

The importance of this story is to enable people to wonder what their family, organization, or community would be like if it were gift-based and not just skill-based.

One time, I did this process with a group in our local high school. We went around the circle and we got to this young man, and he told the story of his names well and the story of his community well, but when it came time to tell the story of his gift, he asked, "What, Miss? What kind gift you think I get, eh? I stay in this special ed class and I get a hard time read and I cannot do that math. And why you make me shame for, ask me that kind question? What kind gift you have? If I had gift, you think I be here?"

He just shut down and shut up, and I felt really shamed. In all the time I have ever done that, I have never, never shamed anybody before.

Two weeks later, I am in our local grocery store, and I see him down one of those aisles and I see his back and I'm going down there with my cart and I think "Nope I'm not going there." So I start to back up as fast as I can and I'm trying to run away from him. And then he turns around and he sees me, and he throws his arms open, and he says, "Aunty! I have been thinking about you, you know. Two weeks I have been thinking: 'What my gift? What my gift?'"

I say "OK bruddah, so what's your gift?"

He says, "You know, I've been thinking, thinking, thinking. I cannot do that math stuff and I cannot read so good, but Aunty, when I stay in the ocean, I can call the fish, and the fish he come, every time. Every time I can put food on my family table. Every time. And sometimes when I stay in the ocean and the Shark he come, and he look at me and I look at him and I tell him, 'Uncle I not going take plenty fish. I just going to take one, two fish, just for my family. All the rest I leave for you.' And so the Shark he say, 'Oh, you cool, brother.' And I tell the Shark, 'Uncle, you cool.' And the Shark, he go his way and I go my way."

And I look at this boy and I know what a genius he is, and I mean, certifiable. But in our society, the way schools are run, he is rubbish. He is totally destroyed, not appreciated at all. So when I talked to his teacher and the principal of the school, I asked them what would his life have been like if this curriculum were gift-based? If we were able to see the gift in each of our children and taught around that gift? What would happen if our community was gift-based? If we could really understand what the gift of each of our communities were, and really began to support that?

CHAPTER 15

Heal, Don't Punish

Fania Davis

Tommy, an agitated 14-year-old high school student in Oakland, California, was in the hallway cursing out his teacher at the top of his lungs. A few minutes earlier, in the classroom, he'd called her a "bitch" after she twice told him to lift his head from the desk and sit up straight. Eric Butler, the school coordinator for Restorative Justice for Oakland Youth (RJOY) heard the ruckus and rushed to the scene. The principal also heard it and appeared. Though Butler tried to engage him in conversation, Tommy was in a rage and heard nothing. He even took a swing at Butler that missed. Grabbing the walkie-talkie to call security, the principal angrily told Tommy he would be suspended.

"I don't care if I'm suspended. I don't care about anything," Tommy defiantly responded. Butler asked the principal to allow him to try a restorative approach with Tommy instead of suspending him.

Butler immediately began to try to reach Tommy's mother. This angered Tommy even more. "Don't call my momma. She ain't gonna do nothing. I don't care about her either."

"Is everything OK?" The concern in Butler's voice produced a noticeable shift in Tommy's energy.

"No, everything is not OK."

"What's wrong?" Butler asked. Tommy was mistrustful and wouldn't say anything else. "Man, you took a swing at me, I didn't fight back. I'm just trying my best to keep you in school. You know I'm not trying to hurt you. Come to my classroom. Let's talk."

They walked together to the restorative justice room. Slowly, the boy began to open up and share what was weighing on him. His mom, who had been successfully doing drug rehabilitation, had relapsed. She'd been out for three days. The 14-year-old was going home every night to a motherless household and two younger siblings. He had been holding it together as best he could, even getting his brother and sister breakfast and getting them off to school. He had his head down on the desk in class that day because he was exhausted from sleepless nights and worry.

After the principal heard Tommy's story, he said, "We were about to put this kid out of school, when what he really deserved was a medal."

Butler tracked down Tommy's mother, did some prep work, and facilitated a restorative justice circle with her, Tommy, the teacher, and the principal. Using a technique borrowed from indigenous traditions, each had a turn with the talking piece, an object that has a special meaning to the group. It moves from person to person, tracing a circle. The person holding the talking piece is the only one talking, and the holder speaks with respect and from the heart.

Everyone else in the circle listens with respect and from the heart.

As Tommy held the talking piece, he told his story. On the day of the incident, he had not slept, and he was hungry and scared. He felt the teacher was nagging him. He'd lost it. Tommy apologized. He passed the talking piece to his teacher and heard her story.

Earlier in the year another student had assaulted her. She was terrified it was about to happen again with Tommy. After the incident with Tommy, as much as she loved teaching, she had considered quitting. Tommy apologized again for the outburst and offered to make amends by helping her with after-school chores for the next few weeks. The teacher agreed to show more compassion in the future if she noticed a student's head down on the desk.

Taking responsibility, Tommy's mother apologized to her son and all present. She rededicated herself to treatment and was referred to the campus drug rehabilitation counselor. After the circle and with follow-up, Tommy's family life, grades, and behavior improved. The teacher remained at the school.

Restoration, Not Punishment

Nelson Mandela's adage, "I destroy my enemies when I make them my friends" captures the profoundly inclusive nature of restorative justice (RJ). The hallmark of RJ is intentionally bringing together people with seemingly diametrically opposed viewpoints—particularly people who have harmed with people who have been harmed—in a carefully prepared face-to-face encounter where everyone listens and speaks with respect and from the heart no matter their differences. The talking piece is a powerful equalizer, allowing everyone's voice to be heard and honored, whether that of a police officer, a judge, or a 14-year-old youth.

If the school had responded in the usual way by suspending Tommy, harm would have been replicated, not healed. Punitive justice asks only what rule or law was broken, who did it, and how they should be punished. It responds to the original harm with more harm. Restorative justice asks who was harmed, what are the needs and obligations of all affected, and how do they figure out how to heal the harm.

Had punitive discipline ruled the day, Tommy's story would have gone unheard and his needs unmet. Had he been suspended, Tommy's chances of engaging in violence and being incarcerated would have dramatically increased. Suspension likely would have exacerbated harm on all sides—to Tommy, his teacher, his family, and ultimately, his community. His teacher would have been deprived of hearing Tommy's story. She might have quit teaching and remained trapped in trauma.

If Tommy had been suspended and left unsupervised—as most suspended students are—he would have been behind in his coursework when he returned. Trapped in an under-resourced school without adequate tutoring and counseling, Tommy would have had a hard time catching up. According to a national study, he would have been three times more likely to drop out by 10th grade than students who had never been suspended.

Worse, had Tommy dropped out, his chances of being incarcerated later in life would have tripled. According to a study by the Centers for Disease Control, a student's sense of belonging to a high school community is a top protective factor against violence and incarceration. Seventy-five percent of the nation's inmates are high school dropouts.[2]

Getting Kids out of the Pipeline

The school-to-prison pipeline refers to the alarming national trend of punishing and criminalizing our youth instead of educating and nurturing them. Exclusionary discipline policies such as suspensions, expulsions, and school-based arrests are increasingly being used to address even the most minor infractions. According to data from the U.S. Office of Civil Rights, black students are three times more likely to be suspended than their white counterparts for comparable offenses.[3]

In addition to convening restorative justice circles like Tommy's, RJOY also uses circles proactively to deepen relationships and create a school culture of connectivity, thereby reducing the likelihood that harm will occur.

Today, at one of the RJOY school sites, student suspensions decreased 74 percent after two years and referrals for violence fell 77 percent after one year. Racial disparity in discipline was eliminated.

Young high school students in Oakland with failing grades and multiple incarcerations who were not expected to graduate not only graduate but achieve 3.0-plus GPAs. Some have become class valedictorians. Girls who have been long-time enemies become friends after sitting in a peacemaking circle. Instead of fighting, students come into the restorative justice room and ask for a talking piece and circle. Youth report they are doing circles at home with their families. High school graduates are returning to their schools to ask for circles to address conflict outside the school.

Oakland is considered one of the most violent cities in the nation. However, today hundreds of Oakland students are learning a new habit. Instead of resorting to violence, they are being empowered to engage in restorative processes that bring together persons harmed with persons responsible for harm in a safe and respectful space, promoting dialogue, accountability, a deeper sense of community, and healing.

CHAPTER 16

The Hidden Treasures in Your Neighborhood

John McKnight and Peter Block

When family members do not work or live well together we sometimes call the family dysfunctional. But the real challenge to the family is that it has lost its job.

Consumer society has put an end to the functional family. We normally think of consumerism as buying stuff we want but don't need, but it runs deeper than that. The essential promise of consumerism is that all of what is fulfilling or needed in life can be purchased—from happiness to healing, from love to laughter, from raising a child to caring for someone at the end of life. What was once the task of the family and the neighborhood is now outsourced. Aunt Martha is forgetful? Little Arthur is restless? Get them a diagnosis and a prescription.

The cost of this outsourcing is that the family has lost its capacity to manage the necessities it traditionally provided—to function as the primary place to raise children, sustain health, care for the vulnerable, and ensure economic security. Moreover, the community and neighborhood, which used to provide the extended support system to help the family in all these key functions, are no longer competent. We expect the school, coaches, agencies, social workers, probation officers, sitters, and day care to raise our children. The usefulness that used to reside in the neighborhood is now provided by the marketplace.

Outsiders Raising Children

"It takes a village to raise a child" is an African saying repeated as a matter of faith by American leaders of all persuasions. Yet most of our children are not raised by a village. Instead, they are raised by teachers and counselors in school, youth workers and coaches out of school, juvenile therapists and corrections officials if they are deviant, television and computers and cell phones if they have spare time, and McDonald's if they are hungry. What this means is that the space that the family and neighborhood once filled has been sold and is now filled with paid professionals, electronic toys, and marketing.

Until the 20th century, the basic idea in rearing children was that they become effective grownups by connecting with productive adults and learning from them the community's skills, traditions, and customs. Youth learned from the community and had jobs to do: caring for the elderly and young, doing errands for the household, helping with food. When they became adults, they were equipped to care both for the next generation and for those who had cared for them.

What we now know is that the most effective local communities are those where neighborhoods and citizens have reclaimed their traditional roles. The research on this point is decisive. Where there are "thick" community connections, there is positive child development. Health improves, the environment is sustained, and people are safer and have a better local economy.

Awakening the Power of Families and Neighborhoods

Creating a more community-based way to live and find satisfaction, even when surrounded by a consumer culture, requires only that we act as if each of us has what we need. We have the gifts, structures, and capacities to substitute for our habit of consumption. We can decide to shift our attention toward building the functions of our family and neighborhood.

Here is a story of how this works, drawn from the real-life experiences of families from neighborhoods around the world that we have worked with.

Naomi Alessio and Jackie Barton were walking through the neighborhood, talking about being overwhelmed with work, meals, lessons, school, and especially the kids. Except, Naomi noted, her son, Theron, had begun to turn around.

Last summer, when Theron looked through the open door of the metalworking shop Mr. Thompson had set up in his garage, the old man invited him in. Something clicked. Theron began to stop by every day, and he started bringing home metal pieces he'd learned to make.

Naomi could see Theron change. He was proud of what he made—Mr. Thompson even paid him to make a few things. Naomi said she'd finally stopped worrying about what Theron was doing after school. Jackie admitted that her son, Alvin, was in trouble, and she asked Naomi if there might be someone in the neighborhood whose skills would interest Alvin.

They knew that Gerald Lilly was into fishing, and that Sam Wheatley was a saxophonist, but that was about it. They decided to ask all the men in the neighborhood about their interests and skills. Mr. Thompson agreed to go with them.

It took three weeks to visit all the men on the block. When they were done, they were amazed at what they had found: men who knew juggling, barbecuing, bookkeeping, hunting, haircutting, bowling, investigating crimes, writing poems, fixing cars, weightlifting, choral singing, teaching dogs tricks, mathematics, praying, and how to play trumpet, drums, and sax. They found enough talent for all the kids in the neighborhood to tap into.

Three of the men they met—Charles Wilt, Mark Sutter, and Sonny Reed—joined Naomi, Jackie, and Mr. Thompson in finding out what the kids on the block were interested in learning.

When they got together after interviewing the kids, Mark talked about a boy he met who knew about computers. Why not ask all the kids what they knew about? Then they could match adults to the kids, just as they planned to match up the kids with the grown-ups. When they were done, they found they had 22 things the young people knew that might interest some adults on the block.

The six neighbors named themselves the Matchmakers and, as they got more experience, they began to connect neighbors who shared the same interests. The gardeners' team shared growing tips and showed four families how to create gardens—even on a flat rooftop. Several people who were worried about the bad economy created a website where neighbors who knew about available work could post job openings. To give it some flair, they found people in the neighborhood to take photos for the site and gradually opened it up for all sorts of neighborhood uses.

Jolene Cass, for instance, posted one of her poems on the website and asked if there were other poets on the block. It turned out there were three. They began to have coffee, share their writing, and post their poems online.

Eleven adults and kids formed the Block Band, and neighborhood singers formed a choir led by Sarah Ensley, an 80-year-old woman who'd been singing all her life.

Charles Dawes, a police officer, formed a team of adults and young people to make the block a safe haven for everyone.

Libby Green had lived on the block for 74 years. The Matchmakers got two neighborhood teenagers, Lenore Manse and Jim Caldwell, to write down her stories about the neighborhood and post them on the website.

Then Lenore decided to write family histories for everyone on the block, and persuaded Jim and her best friend, Lannie Eaton, to help her record the histories and round up photos to go along with them.

Charles Wilt suggested a way for the Matchmakers to welcome newcomers to the neighborhood and begin to connect them with their neighbors: give them a copy of the block history and get information about the new family's history, skills, and interests.

Three years later, at the annual block party, Jackie Barton summed up what the neighborhood had accomplished:

"What we have done is broken all the lines. We broke the lines between the men. We broke the lines between the women. Then the lines were broken between the men and the women. And best of all, the lines were broken between the adults and the children and between all of us and our seniors. All the lines are broken; we're all connected. We're a real community now."

Seeing the Abundance in the Neighborhood

The story has the elements of what we can call a competent neighborhood. Creating competence starts with making visible the gifts of everyone in the neighborhood—the families, the young people, the old people, the vulnerable people, the troublesome people. Everyone. We do this not out of altruism, but to create the elements of a satisfying life.

This thickens the social fabric. It makes the community's gifts more widely available in support of the family. If we do it, even in small way, we find that much of what we once purchased is at hand: carpentry, Internet knowledge, listening, driving a truck, math, auto repair, organizing ability, gardening, haircutting, wallpapering, making videos, babysitting, house painting, accounting, soccer coaching, artistic abilities, cooking, fitness knowledge, sitting with the old or the ill, health remedies, sewing. And some of those things will come from the elderly, the young, the isolated, and the unemployed.

These local connections can give the modern family what the extended family once provided: a place with a strong culture of kin, friends, and neighbors.

When we become competent again and have families reclaim their functions, we see emerging from our community culture those essential qualities of a satisfying life: kindness, generosity, cooperation, forgiveness, and the ability to live with our common fallibilities. These will all be given a home and nurtured by families who have reclaimed their function.

CHAPTER 17

How to Design Your Neighborhood for Happiness

Jay Walljasper

iology is destiny, declared Sigmund Freud.
But if Freud were around today, he might say "design is destiny"—especially after taking a stroll through most modern cities.

The way we design our communities plays a huge role in how we experience our lives. Neighborhoods built without sidewalks, for instance, mean that people walk less and therefore enjoy fewer spontaneous encounters, which is what instills a spirit of community to a place. A neighborly sense of the commons is missing.

You don't have to be a therapist to realize that this creates lasting psychological effects. It thwarts the connections between people that encourage us to congregate, cooperate, and work for the common good. We retreat into ever more privatized existences.

One of the notable solutions to this problem is New Urbanism,[4] an architectural movement to build new communities (and revitalize existing ones) by maximizing opportunities for social exchange: public plazas, front porches, corner stores, coffee shops, neighborhood schools, narrow streets, and, yes, sidewalks.

But while New Urbanism is making strides at the level of the neighborhood, we still spend most of our time at home, which today means seeing no one other than our nuclear family. How could we widen that circle just a bit? Cooperative living and cohousing communities are gaining popularity, especially among young people. Yet, millions more people are looking for more informal arrangements with neighbors, where they share more than a property line.

That's an idea Seattle-area architect Ross Chapin has explored for many years, and now showcases in an inspiring book, *Pocket Neighborhoods: Creating a Small-Scale Community in a Large-Scale World.*[5]

He believes that groupings of four to 12 households make an ideal community "where meaningful 'neighborly' relationships are fostered." But even here, design shapes our destiny. Chapin explains that strong connections between neighbors develop most fully and organically when everyone shares some "common ground."

That can be a semi-public space, as in the pocket neighborhoods Chapin designs in the Seattle area. They look like grassy patches of paradise, where kids scamper, flowers bloom, and neighbors stop to chat.

But Chapin points out these commons can take many different forms—an apartment building in Cambridge, Massachusetts, with a shared backyard; a group of neighbors in Oakland who tore down their backyard fences to create a commons; neighbors on a block in Baltimore who turned their alley into a public commons; or the residential pedestrian streets found in Manhattan Beach, California, and all around Europe.

Five Ways to Meet Your Neighbors

Ross Chapin

1. **Put a picnic table and vegetable garden in the front yard.** See what happens when you eat supper out front. It's likely you'll strike up a conversation with a neighbor, so invite them to bring a dish to share. Build a raised bed for veggies and plant edible landscaping and fruit trees. Break your boundaries by inviting your neighbors to share your garden.

2. **Organize summer potluck street parties.** Claim the street, gather the lawn chairs, and fire up the hibachi! Take over the otherwise off-limits street as a space to draw neighbors together.

3. **Put up a book-lending cupboard.** Collect your old reads and share them with passersby in a cupboard mounted next to the sidewalk out front.

4. **Build resilience together.** Create a neighborhood survey of assets, skills, and needs for times of crisis. Frame it around "emergency preparedness," but watch how it cultivates community.

5. **Be a good neighbor.** It's easy to focus on your own needs and concerns, but a slight shift in outlook can make a big difference in the day-to-day lives in a neighborhood. Check in on your elderly neighbor if her curtains aren't raised in the morning. On a hot summer day, put out a pitcher of ice lemonade for passersby, or a bowl of cool water for dogs on walks.

The benefits of living in such a community go further than you might imagine. I lived in one while in graduate school—a rundown 1886 row house with a common courtyard near the University of Minnesota campus. At no other time in my life have I become such close friends with my neighbors. We shared impromptu afternoon conversations at the picnic table and parties that went into the early hours of the morning under Italian lights we strung from the trees.

When the property was sold to a speculator who jacked up the rents to raise capital for the eventual demolition of the building, we organized a rent strike. And we won, which would never have happened if we had not already forged strong bonds with each other. Because the judge ruled that the landlord could not raise our rents until he fixed up the building, he abandoned plans to knock it down. It still stands today, and I still remain in contact with some of the old gang that partied in the courtyard.

CHAPTER 18

Lessons in Gratitude From
a Pay-It-Forward Restaurant

Pavithra Mehta

Imagine a restaurant where there are no prices on the menu; a place where the meal is served as a gift by volunteers, and at the end of it guests receive a bill for a total of $0.00.

The bill comes with a note that explains their meal was a gift from someone who came before them. If they wish to pay it forward, they can make a contribution for someone who comes after them and help keep the circle going. This restaurant is called Karma Kitchen—and it actually exists.

When the other founders and I started in 2007 in Berkeley, California, we had no idea whether our project would sink or float. But more than six years later Karma Kitchen is still going strong. It has served more than 30,000 meals and now has chapters in half a dozen cities around the world. And it is all sustained by gratitude.

It baffles people to know that Karma Kitchen has no tracking systems—we don't monitor how much individual tables receive and how much they give. Instead, we just focus on giving everyone a genuine experience of generosity.

Karma Kitchen works on the deceptively simple premise that the heart that fills, spills. The nature of gratitude is to overflow its banks and circulate. It does not stand still. But remove that ineffable quality from the equation, and the virtuous cycle breaks down.

The sociologist Georg Simmel called gratitude "the moral memory of mankind."[6] It serves to connect us to each other in small, real, and human ways. Remove it from the fabric of our lives, and all relationships become an endless series of soulless transactions. We become more prone to a sense of entitlement and less available to a sense of life's wonder and mystery. But when we receive something as a gift as opposed to a purchase, we drop out of our patterns of constant calculation. We step out of the realm of price tags and into the realm of the priceless. This is an important shift.

What Gratitude Has Taught Us

At Karma Kitchen, the fact that there is no way to know who is in the chain before you paid for your meal—and no way of knowing who exactly will receive your contribution—makes it quietly revolutionary. It gently shakes people out of our habitual quid pro quo mindset. It is a system that transcends any one person's control and invites trust in the cycle of the whole. Gratitude is what bolsters the spirit to take that leap of faith. In this context every contribution becomes an act of profound trust. That kind of trust builds a web of resilience. It is what turns a group of people into an actual community.

Gratitude is a creative state, and Karma Kitchen guests and volunteers have illustrated this in many ways. In addition to the monetary contributions from guests that keep the wheels of the restaurant turning, Karma Kitchen has witnessed thousands of other spontaneous offerings—everything from songs, poems, and artwork to exquisite magazines and inspiring DVDs that are made available to all on our "Kindness Table."

But perhaps even more important than what transpires at the restaurant is what happens outside its walls. Gratitude does not recognize strict boundaries, and once ignited it asserts itself in the rhythm of our daily lives. It makes us kinder and more compassionate, more willing and ready to act on our impulses for good. As one guest-turned-volunteer put it, "I've realized Karma Kitchen has turned me into the kind of person who now stops when I see someone with a flat tire on the highway."

CHAPTER 19

Everything I Need to Know About Happiness, I Learned in the Forest

Vandana Shiva

It is from the Himalayan forests and ecosystems that I learned most of what I know about ecology. My father was a forest conservator, and my mother became a farmer after fleeing the tragic partition of India and Pakistan. In the 1970s, when I was a young adult, peasant women from my home region of India in the Garhwal Himalaya began to defend the forests there. Logging had led to landslides and floods, and scarcity of water, fodder, and fuel. The women declared that they would hug the trees, and the loggers would have to kill them before killing the trees.

One of their dramatic protests took place in the Himalayan village of Adwani in 1977, when a village woman named Bachni Devi led resistance against her own husband, who had obtained a contract to cut trees. When officials arrived at the forest, the women held up lighted lanterns although it was broad daylight. The forester asked them to explain. The women replied, "We have come to teach you forestry." He retorted, "You foolish women, how can you prevent tree-felling by those who know the value of the forest? Do you know what forests bear? They produce profit and resin and timber."

The women sang back in chorus:

> *What do the forests bear?*
> *Soil, water, and pure air.*
> *Soil, water, and pure air*
> *Sustain the Earth and all she bears.*

When I became a volunteer for the movement to save these forests, I learned about biodiversity and biodiversity-based living economies. The protection of both has become my life's mission. The failure to understand biodiversity and its many functions is at the root of the impoverishment of nature and culture.

The Dead-Earth Worldview

The war against the Earth began with the idea that humans are separate from nature. Its contemporary seeds were sown when the living Earth was transformed into dead matter to facilitate the Industrial Revolution. Monocultures replaced diversity. "Raw materials" and "dead matter" replaced a vibrant Earth. Terra Nullius (the empty land, ready for occupation regardless of the presence of indigenous peoples) replaced Terra Madre (Mother Earth).

This philosophy goes back to Francis Bacon, called the father of modern science, who said that science and the inventions that result do not "merely exert a gentle guidance over nature's course; they have the power to conquer and subdue her, to shake her to her foundations."[7]

Robert Boyle, the famous 17th-century chemist and a governor of the Corporation for the Propagation of the Gospel Among the New England Indians, was clear that he wanted to rid native people of their ideas about nature. He attacked their perception of nature "as a kind of goddess" and argued that "the veneration, wherewith men are imbued for what they call nature, has been a discouraging impediment to the empire of man over the inferior creatures of God."[8]

The domination images created by Bacon and other leaders of the scientific revolution replaced those of the nurturing Earth, removing a cultural constraint on the exploitation of nature. "One does not readily slay a mother, dig into her entrails for gold, or mutilate her body," philosopher and historian Carolyn Merchant writes.[9]

What Nature Teaches

Today, at a time of multiple crises intensified by globalization, we need to move away from the paradigm of nature as dead matter. We need to move to an ecological paradigm, and for this, the best teacher is nature herself.

This is the reason I started the Earth University/Bija Vidyapeeth at Navdanya's farm.

The Earth University teaches Earth Democracy, which is the freedom for all species to evolve within the web of life, and the freedom and responsibility of humans, as members of the Earth family, to recognize, protect, and respect the rights of other species. Earth Democracy is a shift from anthropocentrism to ecocentrism. And since we all depend on the Earth, Earth Democracy translates into human rights to food and water, to freedom from hunger and thirst.

Because the Earth University is located at Navdanya, a biodiversity farm, participants learn to work with living seeds, living soil, and the web of life. Participants include farmers, school children, and people from across the world.

The Poetry of the Forest

The Earth University is inspired by Rabindranath Tagore, India's national poet and a Nobel Prize laureate.

Tagore started a learning center in Shantiniketan in West Bengal, India, as a forest school, both to take inspiration from nature and to create an Indian cultural renaissance.

The school became a university in 1921, growing into one of India's most famous centers of learning.

Today, just as in Tagore's time, we need to turn to nature and the forest for lessons in freedom.

In "The Religion of the Forest," Tagore wrote about the influence that the forest dwellers of ancient India had on classical Indian literature. The forests are sources of water and the storehouses of a biodiversity that can teach us the lessons of democracy—of leaving space for others while drawing sustenance from the common web of life. Tagore saw unity with nature as the highest stage of human evolution.[10]

In his essay "Tapovan" (Forest of Purity), Tagore writes: "Indian civilization has been distinctive in locating its source of regeneration, material and intellectual, in the forest, not the city.... The culture that has arisen from the forest has been influenced by the diverse processes of renewal of life, which are always at play in the forest, varying from species to species, from season to season, in sight and sound and smell. The unifying principle of life in diversity, of democratic pluralism, thus became the principle of Indian civilization."[11]

In Tagore's writings, the forest was not just the source of knowledge and freedom; it was the source of beauty and joy, of art and aesthetics, of harmony and perfection. It symbolized the universe.

In "The Religion of the Forest," the poet says that our frame of mind "guides our attempts to establish relations with the universe either by conquest or by union, either through the cultivation of power or through that of sympathy."[12]

The forest teaches us union and compassion.

The forest also teaches us enoughness: as a principle of equity, how to enjoy the gifts of nature without exploitation and accumulation. Tagore quotes from the ancient texts written in the forest: "Know all that moves in this moving world as enveloped by God; and find enjoyment through renunciation, not through greed of possession."[13]

The end of consumerism and accumulation is the beginning of the joy of living.

The conflict between greed and compassion, conquest and cooperation, violence and harmony that Tagore wrote about continues today. And it is the forest that can show us the way beyond this conflict.

The Wild Geese

—Wendell Berry

Horseback on Sunday morning,
harvest over, we taste persimmon
and wild grape, sharp sweet
of summer's end. In time's maze
over fall fields, we name names
that went west from here, names
that rest on graves. We open
a persimmon seed to find the tree
that stands in promise,
pale, in the seed's marrow.
Geese appear high over us,
pass, and the sky closes. Abandon,
as in love or sleep, holds
them to their way, clear,
in the ancient faith: what we need
is here. And we pray, not
for new earth or heaven, but to be
quiet in heart, and in eye
clear. What we need is here.[14]

10 Ways Sustainable Happiness
Can Change the World

Happiness is what most of us would like for ourselves. But sustainable happiness is also good medicine for a world beset by war, poverty, and the climate crisis.

When we choose sustainable happiness...

1. **We drop our identities as consumers and become much more.** We no longer allow our sense of self-worth to be defined by what we buy and how our possessions or accomplishments compare with those of our peers. We get free of the vicious cycle of debt and overwork (if we're poor or middle class) and excess (if we're wealthy). Our minds and hearts are unleashed, and we can realize our potential as complex and extraordinary beings living on a fragile planet.

2. **We reclaim our time for things and people that matter.** Buying, maintaining, repairing, storing, and using lots of stuff gobbles up time, as does reaching for titles or superficial symbols of prestige. Research tells us we are far more likely to build real happiness for ourselves, our loved ones, and the greater world by maintaining meaningful relationships, making a

contribution to our communities, and expressing gratitude for the contributions others make.

3. **We become freer and more powerful.** When we are out of debt; when we don't allow advertisers to define us; when we take up our rights as citizens (with or without documents) and collaborate, we become free and powerful. Instead of being the pawns in someone else's game, we become protagonists of history. Together with our families, neighbors, and fellow citizens we can create a world that works, not just for the 1 percent, but for all.

4. **We avoid fueling sweatshops and environmentally degrading companies.** Consumer demand for cheap stuff—along with the corporate drive for profit—fuels the push to maintain low wages and cut corners on working conditions. When we shift to buying less and buying responsibly, we shift away from this degrading economy.

5. **We help a strong, sustainable economy take root.** When we buy high-quality, locally made, and fairly traded stuff, we help support an economy that offers everyone a decent standard of living. Sustainable economies are locally based, and so they strengthen connections with our neighbors, create higher-quality and more rewarding jobs, and keep our community resources local.

6. **We contribute to a more equitable distribution of wealth.** Reducing inequality alleviates poverty, crime, illness, and isolation. And a more equitable society has more trust and greater solidarity. Instead of living separately, divided by class, we all benefit from strong communities in which no one is left behind.

7. **We protect the web of life.** And that means living as though there will be a tomorrow. Reducing fossil fuel extraction, deforestation, and mining means healthier oceans, cleaner air and water, less dependence on the industrial food system—and a happier planet. When life thrives, we thrive—emotionally, spiritually, and physically. When we no longer see ourselves as separate, we cease to destroy the life that sustains us and we experience the vitality and awe of an extraordinary living planet.

8. **We strengthen our neighborhoods and communities.** When we grow and make more of our own stuff, or buy, barter, and share it with our neighbors, we encourage neighborliness and connection. Also, when we can afford to spend less time on the job, we have more time to spend at home. We can take the time to sit and talk—and listen.

9. **We reduce trauma and contribute to healing.** Instead of condemning those who have been traumatized by war, abuse, and poverty, and punishing them when they act out, we work to resolve the unbearable pain at the root of many social ills. We gain the skills of mindfulness and equanimity to help ourselves and each other during hard times. When we are healed instead of punished, our gifts are unleashed, and we become productive, creative members of the Beloved Community.

10. **We are each valued for the precious and unique gift we offer to the world.** Our energy, passion, ingenuity, and creativity are freed up, and our contribution is valued. We do work at a job that fits our gifts and passions, whether or not it contributes to economic growth. When we are less hampered and disillusioned by mindless work, we experience more clarity about our calling.

Sustainable happiness is contagious. Plant the seeds at home or at work and you might find that the effects ripple out into unexpected outbreaks of joy, creativity, and the innovations that just might bring about a more just and sustainable world.

Visit www.yesmagazine.org/happiness-book for more powerful ideas and practical actions.

Notes

Introduction

1. Kline Hunnicut, Benjamin. "The End of Shorter Hours." *Labor History* (Summer 1984). 373–404. http://www.uiowa.edu/~lsa/bkh/lla/eosh .htm.

2. Gore, Al. *The Future: Six Drivers of Global Change.* New York: Random House, 2013. 158. http://goo.gl/Gi51Nc.

3. Committee on Recent Economic Changes of the President's Conference on Unemployment, *Recent Economic Changes in the United States* (National Bureau of Economic Research, 1929).

4. Gore, Al. *The Future: Six Drivers of Global Change.* New York: Random House, 2013. 158. http://goo.gl/Gi51Nc.

5. Perry, Mark. "Today's new homes are 1,000 square feet larger than in 1973, and the living space per person has doubled over the last 40 years." *Carpe Diem* (June 6, 2014). http://www.aei-ideas.org/2014/02 /todays-new-homes-are-1000-square-feet-larger-than-in-1973-and -the-living-space-per-person-has-doubled-over-last-40-years.

6. "Advertising to Children and Teens: Current Practices." *Common Sense Media* (Spring 2013). https://www.commonsensemedia.org /research/advertising-to-children-and-teens-current-practices.

7. Stelter, Brian. "8 Hours a Day Spent on Screens, Study Finds." *New York Times*, March 29, 2009. http://www.nytimes.com/2009/03/27 /business/media/27adco.html.

8. Gerbner, G., Gross, L., Morgan, M., Signorielli, N., & Shanahan, J. (2002). In J. Bryant & D. Zillmann (Eds.), Media effects: Advances in theory and research (2nd ed., pp. 43–67). Mahwah, N J: Lawrence Erlbaum Associates, Inc.

9. Pimm, Stuart et al. "The Biodiversity of Species and Their Rates of Extinction, Distribution, and Protection." *Science*, 344 (2014). doi: 10.1126/science.1246752.

10. Kubiszewski, Ida et al. "Beyond GDP: Measuring and Achieving Global Genuine Progress." *Ecological Economics* (April 2013).

11. Gilens, Martin and Benjamin Page, "Testing Theories of American Politics: Elites, Interest Groups, and Average Citizens," *Perspectives on Politics*, April 2013. http://www.princeton.edu/~mgilens/Gilens% 20homepage%20materials/Gilens%20and%20Page/Gilens%20and %20Page%202014-Testing%20Theories%203-7-14.pdf.

12. Reno, Jamie. "Nearly 30% of Vets Treated by V. A. Have PTSD." *The Daily Beast*, October 21, 2012. http://www.thedailybeast.com /articles/2012/10/21/nearly-30-of-vets-treated-by-v-a-have-ptsd.html.

13. Price, Jennifer. "When a Child's Parent has PTSD." U.S. Department of Veterans Affairs. http://www.ptsd.va.gov/professional/treatment /children/pro_child_parent_ptsd.asp.

14. Kilpatrick, Dean G. "The Mental Health Impact of Rape." National Violence Against Women Prevention Research Center, Medical University of South Carolina. http://www.soc.iastate.edu/sapp/rape1.pdf.

15. "Child Maltreatment 2012," *U.S. Department of Health & Human Services.* http://www.acf.hhs.gov/sites/default/files/cb/cm2012.pdf.

16. Williams, Monica. "Can Racism Cause PTSD? Implications for DSM-5." *Psychology Today* (May 20, 2013). http://www.psychology today.com/blog/culturally-speaking/201305/can-racism-cause-ptsd -implications-dsm-5.

17. Sanders, Robert. "Researchers find out why some stress is good for you." *UC Berkeley News Center* (April 16, 2013). https://newscenter .berkeley.edu/2013/04/16/researchers-find-out-why-some-stress-is -good-for-you/.

18. Marmot. M. G. et al. "Inequalities in death—specific explanations of a general pattern?" Mortality decline and widening social inequalities." *Lancet* (1984): 1003–06.

19. Anderson, Cameron, Michael W. Kraus, and Dacher Keltner. "The local-ladder effort: social status and subjective well-being." (2011). http://www.irle.berkeley.edu/workingpapers/110-11.pdf.

20. Kennelly, Stacey. "Happiness Comes From Respect, Not Riches." *YES! Magazine* (August 3, 2012). http://www.yesmagazine.org /happiness/happiness-comes-from-respect-not-riches.

21. Kasser, Tim. "Making a Difference Makes You Happy." *YES! Magazine* (May 5, 2010). http://www.yesmagazine.org/happiness/making-a -difference-makes-you-happy.

22. Novotney, Amy. "Getting back to the great outdoors." *Monitor on Psychology* 39 (2008): 52. http://www.apa.org/monitor/2008/03 /outdoors.aspx.

23. "Exercise is Medicine." *American College of Sports Medicine.* http://exerciseismedicine.org/documents/EIMFactSheet2012_all.pdf.

24. Dunn A. L. 1, Trivedi M. H., Kampert J. B., Clark, C. G., Chambliss, H. O. "Exercise treatment for depression: efficacy and dose response." *American Journal of Preventive Medicine*, January 2005 Vol. 28, Issue 1, p1–8 http://http://www.ajpmonline.org/article/S0749-3797(04)00241 -7/fulltext

25. Frankl, Victor E. *Man's Search for Meaning.* Boston: Beacon Press, 1959.

26. Ruttenberg, Tara. "Wellbeing Economics and Buen Vivir: Development Alternatives for Inclusive Human Security." *PRAXIS: The Fletcher Journal of Human Security* XXVVIII (2013). http://fletcher .tufts.edu/Praxis/~/media/Fletcher/Microsites/praxis/xxviii/article4 _Ruttenberg_BuenVivir.pdf.

27. de Graaf, John and Laura Musikanski. "The Pursuit of Happiness." *Earth Island Journal.* http://www.earthisland.org/journal/index.php /eij/article/the_pursuit_of_happiness.

28. "Gross National Happiness and Development" *The Centre of Bhutan Studies* (2004). http://www.bhutanstudies.org.bt/publicationFiles /ConferenceProceedings/GNHandDevelopment/GNH-I-1.pdf.

29. "Adopting Resolution on Multilingualism, General Assembly Emphasizes Importance of Equality Among Six Official United Nations Languages." *United Nations*. July 19, 2011. http://www.un.org/News /Press/docs/2011/ga11116.doc.htm.

Part One

1. Russell, Bertrand. *Principles of Social Reconstruction*. London: George Allen & Unwin Ltd., 1917.

Chapter 1

This chapter is based on Roman Krznaric's book *How Should We Live? Great Ideas from the Past for Everyday Life* (BlueBridge). It was published on yesmagazine.org in December 2013.

2. Saad, Linda. "U.S. Workers Least Happy With Their Work Stress and Pay." *Gallup*, November 12, 2012. http://www.gallup.com/poll/158723 /workers-least-happy-work-stress-pay.aspx.

3. Kahneman, Daniel and Angus Deaton. "High income improves evaluation of life but not emotional well-being." *Proceedings of the National Academy of Sciences*, August 2010. http://www.pnas.org/content/early /2010/08/27/1011492107.abstract.

4. Sahlins, Marshall. *Stone-Age Economics*. New Jersey: Transaction Publishers, 1974.

5. Matthew 13:12.

6. House, Adrian. *Francis of Assisi: A Revolutionary Life*. New York: Paulist Press, 2003.

7. Shi, David. *The Simple Life: Plain Living and High Thinking in American Culture*. New York: Oxford University Press, 1985.

8. Thoreau, Henry David. *Walden and Civil Disobedience*. New York: Penguin, 1986.

Chapter 2

This chapter originally appeared in "Sustainable Happiness," the Winter 2009 issue of *YES! Magazine*.

9. Lyubomirsky, Sonja. *The How of Happiness: A Scientific Approach to Getting the Life You Want.* New York: Penguin Press, 2008.

10. Kohn, Alfie. "In Pursuit of Affluence, at a High Price." *New York Times,* February 2, 1999. http://www.alfiekohn.org/managing/ipoa.htm.

11. Diener, Ed and Robert Biswas-Diener. *Happiness: Unlocking the Mysteries of Psychological Wealth.* Oxford: Blackwell Publishing Limited, 2008.

12. Ben-Shahar, Tal. *Happier: Learn the Secrets to Daily Joy and Lasting Fulfillment.* New York: McGraw-Hill, 2007.

13. Diener, Ed and Robert Biswas-Diener. *Happiness: Unlocking the Mysteries of Psychological Wealth.* Oxford: Blackwell Publishing Limited, 2008.

14. Emmons, Robert. *Thanks! How the New Science of Gratitude Can Make You Happier.* Boston: Houghton Mifflin Company, 2007.

15. Dunn, Elizabeth and Michael Norton. *Happy Money: The Science of Smarter Spending.* New York: Simon & Schuster, 2014.

Chapter 3

This chapter originally appeared in "The Human Cost of Stuff," the Fall 2013 issue of *YES! Magazine.*

16. Claudio, Luz. "Waste Couture: Environmental Impact of the Clothing Industry." *Environmental Health Perspectives* 115 (September 2007): A449–A454. http://www.ncbi.nlm.nih.gov/pmc/articles/PMC1964887.

17. Leonard, Annie. *The Story of Stuff.* New York: Free Press, 2011.

18. Lacey, Marc. "Across Globe, Empty Bellies Bring Rising Anger." *New York Times,* April 18, 2008. http://nyti.ms/1hKgkBc.

19. Hanauer, Nick and Eric Liu. *The Gardens of Democracy: A New American Story of Citizenship, the Economy, and the Role of Government.* Seattle: Sasquatch Books, 2011.

Chapter 4

This chapter originally appeared on yesmagazine.org in the fall of 2010.

20. Pickett, Kate and Richard Wilkinson. *The Spirit Level: Why Greater Equality Makes Societies Stronger.* New York: Bloomsbury Books, 2009.

Chapter 5

This chapter originally appeared in "How Cooperatives Are Driving the New Economy," the Spring 2013 issue of *YES! Magazine*.

21. Darwin, Charles. *The Descent of Man, and Selection in Relation to Sex.* London: John Murray, 1871.

22. Tomasello, Michael et al. "Two Key Steps in the Evolution of Human Cooperation: The Interdependence Hypothesis," *Current Anthropology,* 53 (2012): 673–686.

23. Hamann, Katharina et al. "Collaboration Encourages Equal Sharing in Children But Not in Chimpanzees." *Nature* 476 (August 18, 2011): 328–331.

Chapter 6

This chapter originally appeared in Akaya Windwood's column in the Rockwood Leadership Institute's newsletter. It was later reposted on yesmagazine.org.

Part Two

1. Frankl, Viktor E. *Man's Search for Meaning.* Boston: Beacon Press, 1959.

Chapter 7

This chapter originally appeared in "Sustainable Happiness," the Winter 2009 issue of *YES! Magazine*.

Chapter 8

This chapter originally appeared on yesmagazine.org in the summer of 2010.

Chapter 9

This chapter is adapted from an article on the blog Change From Within. It appeared on yesmagazine.org in February 2014.

2. "Pornography Statistics," Covenant Eyes, http://www.discernemen .com/fichs/10141.pdf (accessed June 5, 2014).

3. "Pornography Statistics," Family Safe Media, http://familysafemedia
   .com/pornography_statistics.html#anchor7 (accessed June 5, 2014).

4. Let me state clearly that I don't think all porn is bad. I've seen some
   great videos of couples engaging in intimate and respectful sexual
   encounters—of course, these are usually found only on feminist
   porn sites or in the category on mainstream porn sites called "female
   friendly." But I'm not here to judge anyone else for what they choose
   to watch. I'm simply sharing the impacts that porn has had on my life
   and what has changed for me since I've stopped using it.

5. "Erectile Dysfunction and Porn (Part 1)," Your Brain on Porn.
   http://yourbrainonporn.com/erectile-dysfunction-porn-part-1
   (accessed June 5, 2014).

6. Rohr, Richard. *On the Threshold of Transformation: Daily Meditations
   for Men.* Chicago: Loyola Press, 2010.

Chapter 10

This chapter is based on Roman Krznaric's book *How to Find Fulfilling
Work* (Picador). It appeared on yesmagazine.org in May 2013.

7. Saad, Linda. "U.S. Workers Least Happy With Their Work Stress and
   Pay." *Gallup*, November 12, 2012. http://www.gallup.com/poll/158723
   /workers-least-happy-work-stress-pay.aspx.

8. YouTube. "Barry Schwartz: The paradox of choice." Accessed June 9,
   2014. http://youtu.be/VO6XEQIsCoM.

9. Kahneman, Daniel. *Thinking, Fast and Slow.* New York: Farrar, Straus,
   and Giroux, 2013.

10. Williams, John. *Screw Work, Let's Play: How to Do What You Love and
    Get Paid for It.* Upper Saddle River, NJ: FT Press, 2011.

11. Cooper, Cary and Stephen Wood. "Happiness at work: why it counts."
    The Guardian, July 15, 2011. http://www.theguardian.com/money/2011
    /jul/15/happiness-work-why-counts.

12. Gardner, Howard. *Good Work.* New York: Basic Books, 2002.

13. Drayton, Bill. "Everyone's a Changemaker: Social Entrepreneurship's
    Ultimate Goal." *Innovations* (2006). https://www.ashoka.org/files
    /innovations8.5x11FINAL_0.pdf.

14. "Dream job or career nightmare?" *OPP*, 2007. http://www.opp.com.

Chapter 11

This chapter originally appeared in "What Happy Families Know," the Winter 2011 issue of *YES! Magazine*.

Chapter 12

This chapter originally appeared in "What Happy Families Know," the Winter 2011 issue of *YES! Magazine*.

15. Garcia-Prats, Cathy. *Good Families Don't Just Happen: What We Learned from Raising Our Ten Sons and How It Can Work for You.* Adams Media Corporation, 1997.

16. "2011/12 National Survey of Children's Health." *National Center for Health Statistics*, 2012. http://www.childhealthdata.org/browse/survey/results?q=2290&r=1.

17. "The Importance of Family Dinners V." *CASAColumbia*, September 2009. http://www.casacolumbia.org/addiction-research/reports/importance-of-family-dinners-2009.

18. Obama, Barack. "Presidential Proclamation—Family Day." *The White House*, 2010. http://www.whitehouse.gov/the-press-office/2010/09/27/presidential-proclamation-family-day.

19. "2010 family dinners report finds: Teens who have infrequent family dinners likelier to expect to use drugs in the future." *CASAColumbia*, September 2010. http://www.casacolumbia.org/newsroom/press-releases/2010-family-dinners-report-finds.

20. Story, Mary and Dianne Neumark-Sztainer, "A Perspective on Family Meals: Do They Matter?" *Nutrition Today* 40 (November 2005): 261–266.

21. Joseph Durlak et al. "The Impact of Enhancing Students' Social and Emotional Learning: A Meta-Analysis of School-Based Universal Interventions." *Child Development* 82 (January 2011): 405–432.

22. "Longitudinal Associations Between Family Dinner and Adolescent Perceptions of Parent–Child Communication Among Racially Diverse Urban Youth." *Journal of Family Psychology*, 24 (June 2010): 261–270. http://psycnet.apa.org/?&fa=main.doiLanding&doi=10.1037/a0019311.

Chapter 13

The chapter originally appeared on *Greater Good*, the online magazine of The Greater Good Science Center at the University of California, Berkeley. It was published on yesmagazine.org in December 2013.

23. Carter, Christine. "Habits are Everything." Greater Good Science Center, April 16, 2012. http://greatergood.berkeley.edu/raising_happiness /post/habits1 (accessed June 4, 2014).

24. Emmons, Robert. "How Gratitude Can Help You Through Hard Times." Greater Good Science Center, May 13, 2013. http://greatergood .berkeley.edu/article/item/how_gratitude_can_help_you_through _hard_times (accessed June 4, 2014).

25. Marsh, Jason. "The Grateful Dead." Greater Good Science Center, October 11, 2011. http://greatergood.berkeley.edu/article/item/the _grateful_dead (accessed June 4, 2011).

26. Koo, Minkyung et al. "It's a Wonderful Life: Mentally Subtracting Positive Events Improves People's Affective States, Contrary to Their Affective Forecasts." *Journal of Personality and Social Psychology* 95, no. 5 (2008): 1217-1224. http://www.wjh.harvard.edu/~dtg/KOO%20 ALGOE%20WILSON%20GILBERT%20%282008%29.pdf.

27. Marsh, Jason and Robb Willer. "Why Lent Makes People Happy (and Netflix Doesn't)." Greater Good Science Center, March 21, 2013. http://greatergood.berkeley.edu/article/item/why_lent_makes_people _happy_and_netflix_doesnt (accessed June 4, 2014).

28. Kennelly, Stacey. "10 Steps to Savoring the Good Things in Life." Greater Good Science Center, July 23, 2012. http://greatergood.berkeley .edu/article/item/10_steps_to_savoring_the_good_things_in_life (accessed June 4, 2014).

29. Nauman, Emily. "Do Rituals Help Us to Savor Food?" Greater Good Science Center, August 7, 2013. http://greatergood.berkeley.edu/article /item/do_rituals_help_us_to_savor_food (accessed June 4, 2014).

30. Emmons, Robert. "What Gets in the Way of Gratitude?" Greater Good Science Center, November 12, 2013. http://greatergood.berkeley.edu /article/item/what_stops_gratitude (accessed June 4, 2014).

31. Ibid.

32. Gordon, Amie M. "Four Ways to Make the Most of Gratitude on Valentine's Day." Greater Good Science Center, February 12, 2013, http://greatergood.berkeley.edu/article/item/four_ways_to_make _the_most_of_gratitude_on_valentines_day (accessed June 4, 2014).

Part Three

1. King, Martin Luther, Jr. "Facing the Challenge of a New Age." First Annual Institute on Nonviolence and Social Change, Montgomery, Alabama, December 3, 1956.

Chapter 14

This chapter originally appeared in "Sustainable Happiness," the Winter 2009 issue of *YES! Magazine*.

Chapter 15

This chapter originally appeared in "Education Uprising," the Winter 2014 issue of *YES! Magazine*.

2. "School Connectedness: Strategies for Increasing Protective Factors Among Youth." *Department of Health and Human Services*, 2009. http://www.cdc.gov/healthyyouth/protective/pdf/connectedness.pdf.

3. "Data Snapshot: School Discipline." Office for Civil Rights, March 2014. http://www2.ed.gov/about/offices/list/ocr/docs/crdc-discipline -snapshot.pdf.

Chapter 16

This chapter originally appeared in "What Happy Families Know," the Winter 2011 issue of *YES! Magazine*.

Chapter 17

This chapter originally appeared on yesmagazine.org in July 2013.

4. "CNU," Congress for the New Urbanism. http://www.cnu.org (accessed June 4, 2014).

5. Chapin, Ross. *Pocket Neighborhoods: Creating Small-Scale Community in a Large-Scale World.* Newtown, CT: Taunton Press, 2011.

Chapter 18

This chapter originally appeared on yesmagazine.org in November 2013.

6. Wolff, Kurt H. The Sociology of Georg Simmel. "Faithfulness and Gratitude." Free Press, 1950.

Chapter 19

This chapter originally appeared in "What Would Nature Do?" the Winter 2013 issue of *YES! Magazine.* The last section of the chapter was adapted from Vandana Shiva's article "Forests and Freedom," published in the May/June 2011 edition of *Resurgence.*

7. Spedding, J. et al. (eds.) *The Works of Francis Bacon* (Reprinted). Stuttgart: F.F. Verlag, 1963, Vol. V, p. 506.

8. Boyle, Robert. *A Free Inquiry into the Vulgarly Received Notion of Nature; Made in an Essay, Address'd to a Friend.* London, 1686.

9. Marchant, Carolyn. *The Death of Nature: Women, Ecology, and the Scientific Revolution.* San Francisco: Harper & Row, 1980.

10. Tagore, Rabindranath. "The Religion of the Forest," *Creative Unity.* New Delhi, Rupa & Co., 2002.

11. Tagore, Rabindranath. Tapovan (Hindi), Tikamgarh: Gandhi Bhavan, p. 1–2.

12. Tagore, "The Religion of the Forest," p. 45–46.

13. Ibid.

14. Copyright 2012 by Wendell Berry from *New Selected Poems.* Reprinted by permission of Counterpoint.

Index

A

Abundance, resulting from neighborliness, 105–106
and addiction to luxury, 25
abuse, sexual and physical, 9–10
act first, 71
accountability, 43
achievement, 70–71
activism, 34, 38
  consumer-based, 36–38
  happiness and, 11
  political, 11–12
activities, of simple living, 27–28
Actual Café, 62
advertising, 2–4, 20
afflictive mental states, 58
altruism, 31–32, 57, 58
American-style happiness, 2–8
  colonial, and simplicity, 25
  utopian experiments, 26
Anderson, Cameron, 11
Angel, Jen, 20
anger, 56–57
Anthony, St., 25
Aristotle, 53, 72

artistic freedom, 27
attention, 56–58, 63
  to food, 83
attitude, choosing one's, 13
authentic happiness, xiii, 1–3, 8–13, 16, 20 55, 58–59
awareness, of the present moment, 57

B

Bacon, Francis, 116–117
Bednarz, Sal, 61–62
Beloved Community, 88, 89, 91–93, 123
Ben-Shahar, Tal, 30
Bhutan, gross national happiness in, 14–15
biodiversity, 116–117
Biswas-Diener, Robert, 30–31
blessings, counting, 52–53, 83
Block, Peter, 88
Boyle, Robert, 116–117
Bryant, Fred, 83
Buchwald, Art, 28
buen vivir (the good life), 13–14
Bures, Frank, 63

About the Contributors

The chapters in this volume were adapted from articles originally published by *YES! Magazine*. Since its founding in 1996, *YES!* has been reframing the biggest problems of our time in terms of their solutions. Online and in print, *YES!* outlines a path forward with in-depth analysis, tools for citizen engagement, and stories about real people working for a better world. *YES! Magazine* is a nonprofit, ad-free publication and website based near Seattle, Washington. Find additional resources on sustainable happiness at www.yesmagazine.org/happiness-book.

The following authors contributed to this book:

Jen Angel is a writer, publicist, and cupcake baker. She lives in Berkeley, California.

Wendell Berry is a poet, essayist, and fiction writer, who lives and farms in Henry County, Kentucky.

Peter Block is a consultant, speaker, and author of *Flawless Consulting, Stewardship, The Answer to How Is Yes*, and *Community: The Structure of Belonging*. He lives in Cincinnati, Ohio.

Puanani Burgess is a Zen priest, poet, community builder, and Native Hawaiian cultural translator. She is also a member of the board of directors of the Positive Futures Network, publisher of *YES! Magazine.* Pua lives in Wai'anae, Hawai'i.

Ross Chapin is an architect and author of *Pocket Neighborhoods: Creating Small-Scale Community in a Large-Scale World.* He lives on Whidbey Island, Washington.

Fania Davis is the co-founder and executive director of Restorative Justice for Oakland Youth, and she serves as counsel to the International Council of Thirteen Indigenous Grandmothers.

Katherine Gustafson is a freelance writer, journalist, and editor who began her career in the nonprofit sector. She lives in Washington, D.C.

Shannon Hayes is a blogger for *YES! Magazine* and author of four books, including *Radical Homemakers: Reclaiming Domesticity from a Consumer Culture.* She farms with three generations of her family in West Fulton, New York.

Brooke Jarvis is an author and freelance writer. She was formerly a *YES! Magazine* staff editor and is currently a *YES!* contributing editor. Brooke lives in Seattle, Washington.

Eric Michael Johnson is a science writer and creator of "The Primate Diaries," a *Scientific American* blog. He is currently a doctoral student in the history of science at the University of British Columbia.

Erika Kosina is a freelance writer, editor, and communications consultant based in Nevada City, California.

Roman Krznaric is an Australian cultural thinker and author of *How Should We Live? Great Ideas from the Past for Everyday Life, How to Find Fulfilling Work,* and *Empathy: Why It Matters, and How to Get It.* He is a founding faculty member of The School of Life in London.

Annie Leonard is the executive director of Greenpeace USA. She is also an author, a *YES! Magazine* contributing editor, and the creator of the "Story of Stuff" series.

Dan Mahle is program coordinator at the Whidbey Institute, a facilitator with Generation Waking Up, and creator of the blog Wholehearted Masculine (wholeheartedmasculine.org). He lives in Seattle, Washington.

John McKnight is co-director of the Asset-Based Community Development Institute at Northwestern University. He is the author of *The Careless Society* and co-author with Peter Block of *The Abundant Community: Awakening the Power of Families and Neighborhoods.*

Pavithra Methta is a filmmaker and one of the creative forces behind ServiceSpace (www.servicespace.org) and DailyGood. She is also the co-author of *Infinite Vision: How Aravind Became the World's Greatest Business Case for Compassion.*

Matthieu Ricard is a Buddhist monk, French interpreter for the Dalai Lama, and the author of seven books, including *Happiness: A Guide to Developing Life's Most Important Skill.* He is an active member of the Mind and Life Institute, and lives at the Shechen monastery in Nepal.

Vandana Shiva is a world-renowned environmental activist. She has authored more than 20 books and is a *YES! Magazine* contributing editor.

Jeremy Adam Smith is the author of *The Daddy Shift*, founding editor of Shareable.net, and Web editor of *Greater Good*, the online magazine of UC Berkeley's Greater Good Science Center (http://greatergood.berkeley.edu).

Sarah van Gelder is a writer, public speaker, and co-founder and editor in chief of *YES! Magazine*. Sarah edited one of the first books about the Occupy movement, *This Changes Everything: Occupy Wall Street and the 99%* and the anthology *Making Peace: Healing a Violent World*. She lives in Suquamish, Washington.

Jay Walljasper is the author of *All That We Share: A Field Guide to the Commons* and *The Great Neighborhood Book*. He's an editor of On the Commons (www.onthecommons.org) and a *YES! Magazine* contributing editor.

Richard Wilkinson is an epidemiologist and co-author with Kate Pickett of *The Spirit Level: Why More Equal Societies Almost Always Do Better*.

Akaya Windwood is president of the Rockwood Leadership Institute, based in Oakland, California. Akaya speaks and leads trainings nationally and internationally.

Berrett–Koehler
Publishers

Berrett-Koehler is an independent publisher dedicated to an ambitious mission: *Creating a World That Works for All*.

We believe that to truly create a better world, action is needed at all levels—individual, organizational, and societal. At the individual level, our publications help people align their lives with their values and with their aspirations for a better world. At the organizational level, our publications promote progressive leadership and management practices, socially responsible approaches to business, and humane and effective organizations. At the societal level, our publications advance social and economic justice, shared prosperity, sustainability, and new solutions to national and global issues.

A major theme of our publications is "Opening Up New Space." Berrett-Koehler titles challenge conventional thinking, introduce new ideas, and foster positive change. Their common quest is changing the underlying beliefs, mindsets, institutions, and structures that keep generating the same cycles of problems, no matter who our leaders are or what improvement programs we adopt.

We strive to practice what we preach—to operate our publishing company in line with the ideas in our books. At the core of our approach is stewardship, which we define as a deep sense of responsibility to administer the company for the benefit of all of our "stakeholder" groups: authors, customers, employees, investors, service providers, and the communities and environment around us.

We are grateful to the thousands of readers, authors, and other friends of the company who consider themselves to be part of the "BK Community." We hope that you, too, will join us in our mission.

A BK Life Book

This book is part of our BK Life series. BK Life books change people's lives. They help individuals improve their lives in ways that are beneficial for the families, organizations, communities, nations, and world in which they live and work. To find out more, visit **www.bk-life.com**.

Berrett–Koehler
Publishers

A community dedicated to creating
a world that works for all

Dear Reader,

Thank you for picking up this book and joining our worldwide community of Berrett-Koehler readers. We share ideas that bring positive change into people's lives, organizations, and society.

To welcome you, we'd like to offer you a free e-book. You can pick from among twelve of our bestselling books by entering the promotional code **BKP92E** here: http://www.bkconnection.com/welcome.

When you claim your free e-book, we'll also send you a copy of our e-newsletter, the *BK Communiqué*. Although you're free to unsubscribe, there are many benefits to sticking around. In every issue of our newsletter you'll find

- A free e-book
- Tips from famous authors
- Discounts on spotlight titles
- Hilarious insider publishing news
- A chance to win a prize for answering a riddle

Best of all, our readers tell us, "Your newsletter is the only one I actually read." So claim your gift today, and please stay in touch!

Sincerely,

Charlotte Ashlock
Steward of the BK Website

Questions? Comments? Contact me at bkcommunity@bkpub.com.

MIX
From responsible sources
FSC® C113845
www.fsc.org

Certified

Corporation
bcorporation.net